BERLIN

— in your pocket —

MAIN CONTRIBUTOR: **Jack Altman**

PHOTOGRAPH CREDITS

Photos supplied by The Travel Library:

A Cowin back cover, 5, 9, 36, 38, 40, 41, 42, 45, 47, 50, 52, 57, 65, 67, 82, 90, 92, 93, 105, 107, 113, 121; John Denham 95, 116; Richard Glover 7, 63; Michael Klinec front cover, 19, 22, 23, 25, 34, 46, 48, 49(t,b), 51, 53, 55, 56(b), 59, 60, 61, 62, 64, 70, 71, 72(t), 75, 76, 78, 80, 87, 88, 97, 99, 100, 111, 119, 122; Rob Moore 11, 21, 72(b); R Richardson 94; Clare Roberts title page, 14; Jonathan Smith 26, 81; E Zaplatine 15, 56(t), 69, 74, 125.

Other Photos:

Deutsches Theatremuseum, Munich/Bridgeman Art Library, London/New York 28; Gemäldegalerie, Berlin/Bridgeman Art Library, London/New York 85; Historisches Museum der Stadt, Vienna/Bridgeman Art Library, London/New York 16; Prana-Film GMBH, Berlin (Courtesy Kobal) 32; UFA (Courtesy Kobal) 33, 108.

Front cover: Kaiser Wilhelm Memorial Church at night; back cover: Brandenburg Gate; title page: Siegessäule (Victory Column).

MANUFACTURE FRANÇAISE DES PNEUMATIQUES MICHELIN

Place des Carmes-Déchaux – 63000 Clermont-Ferrand (France)

Dépôt légal Avril 98 – ISBN 2-06-652401-8 – ISSN 1272-1689

Printed in Spain 3-98

MICHELIN TYRE PLC
Tourism Department
The Edward Hyde Building
38 Clarendon Road
WATFORD Herts WD1 1SX - UK
☎ (01923) 415000

MICHELIN TRAVEL PUBLICATIONS
Editorial Department
One Parkway South
GREENVILLE, SC 29615
☎ 1-800 423-0485

CONTENTS

INTRODUCTION

The city commands our attention by sheer force of character. Its Prussian past and the assaults of war and hasty reconstruction have left it with none of the easy charm of pretty monuments that attract visitors to other, more romantic, German towns. With a pivotal position between western and eastern Europe, this ever-changing metropolis offers instead a drama, spirit, humour and eccentricity that set it apart from the rest of the country.

Its central role in 20C Europe is seen in buildings that have survived two World Wars and a sometimes almost equally brutal Cold War. The Reichstag inherited by the Weimar Republic from the Kaisers is being boldly restored for the new parliament. Hitler's Olympic Stadium still stands, as do a few admonishing remnants of the Wall that split Berlin in two.

And now the world's leading architects are engaged in an exciting new flurry of construction for the 21C. Prestigious corporate headquarters rise on the wasteland of Potsdamer Platz. In Friedrichstrasse, once a bleak Cold War focus for the US Army's Checkpoint Charlie, luxury shopping galleries, a gleaming new department store, theatres, cafés and restaurants aim to recreate the colourful thoroughfare of Berlin's Golden Twenties. Smart in the sense of clever rather than chic, Berliners may take some time to get used to these new fashionable locations. Even the grand Kurfürstendamm boulevard has always been more brash than elegant.

This is a city of great music and theatre, magnificent museums and constantly

The imposing neo-Baroque Berliner Dom at night, with the Television Tower behind.

innovative art galleries. The avant-garde has always felt at home here. The question now is: will the arrival in force of government officials from Bonn blunt the Berliners' cutting edge, or will it be the Berliners who brighten up the bureaucrats? Bets are on the Berliners.

GEOGRAPHY

The city's landmarks can be picked out from the Television Tower. Here, Unter den Linden cuts through Berlin Mitte, leading to the Tiergarten.

The city is built on swamp and sand. 'Berlin' comes from a word meaning 'damp place', borne out these days more by its abundance of lakes, rivers and canals than by an over wet climate. Newcomers are struck by how green the city is – woodland covers nearly 30 per cent of the metropolitan area. Spread over 889sq km (343 square miles), the city extends some 45km (28 miles) from east to west and 38km (24 miles) from north to south. The population is now nearly 4.5 million.

At the very heart of western Berlin, the great Tiergarten park is bounded by the Spree River and the Landwehr Canal. Out to the south-west, the **Grunewald forest** embraces the sailing lake of **Wannsee** and the **Havel River**, where sandy beaches are as pleasant as any in the smarter resorts on the Baltic or North Sea coasts. To the north are the **Spandau** and **Tegel** forests and Lake Tegel. And now Westerners can rediscover in eastern Berlin the charms of the **Müggelsee** and the parklands of Köpenick and Treptow.

Amid the vast flatlands of the great northern European plain, Berlin's little surprise is Devil's Mountain – **Teufelsberg**. This grassed-over heap of rubble left by the Allies' bombardments in the Second World War is just tall enough, 115m (380ft), to provide Berliners with a couple of ski-slopes in the winter. None of the other hillocks protruding from the city's parks rises any higher.

Since the 19C, Berliners have always been keen to develop and preserve their city's abundant greenery. On the outskirts of town, landscape architects artfully fashioned gardens for Klein-Glienicke Castle, on the

fanta

mid-river Pfaueninsel (Peacock Island) and out at Babelsberg and Potsdam. Long before the word 'ecology' became fashionable the city council fought building speculators to have the streets lined with trees, still a factor in the freshness of the renowned Berliner Luft (Berlin air), even sold in tin-cans as a stunt. Tenement-dwellers' *Laubenkolonien* – private flower and vegetable gardens – are staked out on patches of wasteland (though increasingly coveted by municipal and private developers). And along the path of the Wall, the no-man's-land once known as the Death Strip (*Todesstreife*) has proved an unspoiled environment for wild plants.

HISTORY

The idea of a united Berlin as we know it today is a purely 20C concept. The sprawling modern city is in fact a conglomeration of historically independent communities. Neighbourhoods such as Spandau, Köpenick, Charlottenburg, Wilmersdorf and Schöneberg enjoyed an autonomous existence for centuries, until they were incorporated in 1920 into a new metropolis of 20 districts.

The earliest traces of man's presence, some 11 000 years old, are a few flint weapons and the bones of his prey dug up on the north side of town near Tegel. Archaeologists surmise that they were left by nomadic hunters of reindeer from the southern mountains. Some farming may have begun around 3 000 BC.

Slavs and Germans

A small Germanic community appeared in the 6C AD in the south-west district of Teltow but was absorbed over the next 200 years by colonies of **Slavs** making their home in Spandau on the Havel River and Köpenick on the Spree. Their neighbourhoods – *Kietze* – live on in Berliner parlance as the word for any popular quarter. In 962, **Otto I** became the first emperor of the Holy Roman Empire. By the 12C, the Slavs – prosperous farmers, wood-carvers, weavers and potters – were in turn confronted with the eastward expansion of resourceful **German merchants**. From the Harz region came **Albrecht**, a noble of the Saxon Askanian clan who ousted the Slav prince Jaxa and ruled the region as the first Margrave of Brandenburg. He was nicknamed 'Albert the Bear' and the bear became Berlin's emblem.

In the 13C the city was already divided in two. The fishing village of Cölln was an island in the Spree linked to the mainland by what is today the Mühlendamm embankment. The original township of Berlin itself was over on the River Spree's north bank, a community of innkeepers and

Part of the 13C medieval city wall still remains near the city centre.

carters serving itinerant merchants. Its nucleus was the recently reconstituted Nikolaiviertel, a market place around the Church of St Nicholas.

The **two communities allied** in 1307 to fight robber-barons disrupting their burgeoning commerce on the route between Magdeburg and Poznan. They built a joint town hall on the bridge linking the two townships (today's Rathausbrücke), but each maintained its own council. In 1359 they joined the **Hanseatic League**, designed to promote trade among the merchant cities of the North Sea and the Baltic.

At this time Spandau and Köpenick remained independent townships, though increasingly dependent on their Berlin neighbours for trade in goods from outside the region. Their Slav citizens were also progressively assimilated by the dominant Germanic culture. From the 13C Berlin's small Jewish community made use of Spandau's Jewish cemetery.

Hohenzollerns Come to Stay

Cölln and Berlin continued a life of relative autonomy until 1442 when Brandenburg's **Prince-Elector Frederick II** literally moved in. Exploiting disputes between the two townships, in 1448 he repressed a citizens' revolt known as the **Berliner Unwille** (Berliners' Discontent).

During the Reformation, while other Germans were accepting the religion of their prince, the independent-minded Berliners obliged their **Prince-Elector Joachim II** to adopt Martin Luther's Protestant creed in 1539. Among other things, they no longer wanted to pay Catholic church taxes. They turned a

Franciscan monastery into a publishing house and opened the town's first secular high school (Gymnasium) next door.

The citizens were less fortunate in the **Thirty Years' War** (1618-1648) when their princes tried to play off Protestant and Catholic forces against each other. The unfortified town was ruined, first by the Swedish troops of Gustavus Adolphus, then by the army of the German Emperor. Along with war, plague and famine cut the population in half, reducing it to a mere 5 000.

Prussia's Capital

To pave the way for the capital of a new Prussian state, **Frederick-William**, the **'Great Elector'**, fortified Berlin and set about bolstering the population. His efforts paid

Andreas Schlüter's equestrian statue of Frederick-William, the 'Great Elector', with its plinth of chained prisoners stands in front of Schloss Charlottenburg.

off, for between 1650 and 1709 the population of Berlin increased from 6 000 to 56 000. He welcomed scores of wealthy Jewish refugee families from Vienna in 1671 and, 15 years later, thousands of Protestant Huguenots fleeing France after Louis XIV's revocation of their protective Edict of Nantes. These immigrants – widely travelled merchants, fashionable tailors, skilled jewellers, gourmet cooks and pastry-chefs – brought a distinctive sophistication to Berlin. By 1700 Berlin's population had risen to 37 000.

In 1701, the Great Elector's heir crowned himself **King Frederick I** in (but not yet of) Prussia. His bright and dynamic queen **Sophie Charlotte** pressed the good-natured

Development of Berlin through the centuries.

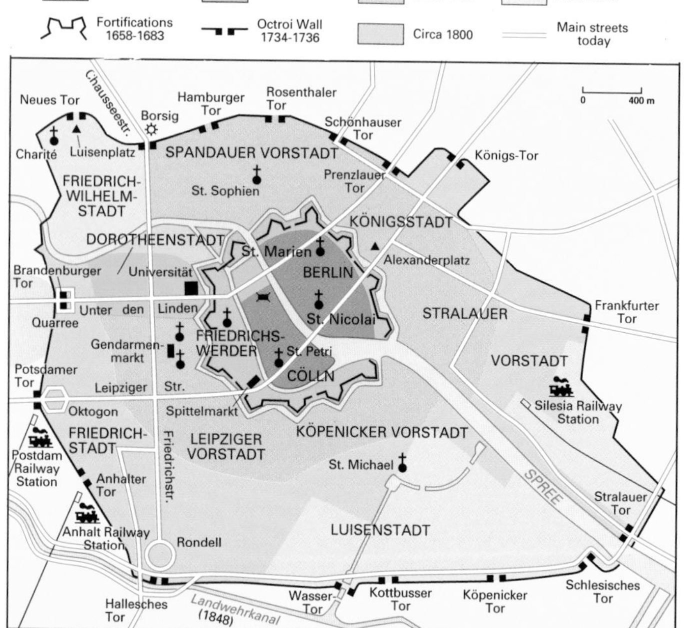

but slow-witted monarch to create academies for the arts and sciences. Architecture flourished, too. Andreas Schlüter's redesigned Berliner Schloss has gone but other Baroque monuments on the Unter den Linden and the Queen's summer palace, Schloss Charlottenburg, still evoke the grace and nobility of the times.

In dour reaction to his pleasure-loving parents, **King Frederick-William I** (1713-1740) tightened everybody's belt. For this vinegary, pious man, austerity began at home. He melted down the palace silver, sold off his coronation robes, preferred beer to wine, and replaced flowers with cabbages in his mother's Charlottenburg gardens. His own royal pleasure-garden – Lustgarten, on today's Museumsinsel – became a military parade-ground. Courtiers dressed all the time, like their chief, later nicknamed the **Sergeant King**, in uniform.

Rebelling in turn against the stifling, resolutely philistine atmosphere of his father's court, **Frederick II** (1740-1786), now king of Prussia, revived Berlin's involvement in the arts and fine buildings. To the Sergeant King's factories for arms and military uniforms he added others for porcelain, silk and velvet. By the time of his death, the population had swelled to 150 000. On the military side, his conquest of Silesia in 1748 won him his title of **Frederick the Great**.

To German Nationhood

Weakened under Frederick II's successors, Prussia's military force was crushed in 1806 by the French armies of **Napoleon** sweeping across eastern Germany. However, the arrogance of the two-year French occupation, underlined by the mortifying confiscation of the proud Quadriga horses atop the Brandenburg Gate, served only to stir German patriotism, and Prussia prepared for its recovery.

Following Napoleon's defeat in 1813, Berlin provided a fertile breeding ground for the new national spirit that the Prussian monarchy found uncomfortably libertarian. Foremost was the city's first university, founded in 1810 with scholar-statesman **Wilhelm von Humboldt** as its driving force.

In 1806 the victorious Napoleon had the Quadriga – symbol of peace – taken to Paris. It was returned a few years later.

Almost as 'dangerous', the **Lesecafés** (reading cafés) attracted intellectuals to discuss political information which they found in foreign and provincial newspapers unhampered by Berlin's press censorship.

The industrial revolution created a new proletariat in a population that in the first half of the 19C doubled to over 400 000. Amid Europe's revolts of 1848, Berlin's uprising brought demonstrators to the Tiergarten and the Berliner Schloss to protest against working and living

The great scholar and statesman Wilhelm von Humboldt sits proudly before the University he championed in 1810.

conditions. Concessions to liberal demands for press freedom and a constitutional monarchy soon gave way to renewed censorship and a police clampdown on political meetings.

In 1862 **Otto von Bismarck** came to power as Prussia's Iron Chancellor. He forged German unity in the next decade with spectacular victories over the Austrians and the French. In 1871 King **William I** was crowned Emperor of the German Reich, with Berlin as its capital. Following the Berlin-Potsdam railway, the bourgeoisie of

King William I, crowned Emperor of the German Reich in 1871.

the Reich's feverishly active **Gründerjahre** (Foundation Years) spread out to the south-west into splendid new villas around the lakes and forest of Grunewald. The boom ushered in mass-circulation newspapers and department stores like the Kaufhaus des Westens (KaDeWe) but was also accompanied by bankruptcies and widespread unemployment.

Mobilisation for the **First World War** was greeted by crowds cheering Kaiser **William II** at the Berliner Schloss, but food rationing and news of massive losses in the trenches soon ended the enthusiasm. In 1916, Rosa Luxemburg and Karl Liebknecht organised opposition in their **Spartacus League**, forerunner of the German Communist Party. In January 1918, a strike of 400 000 Berlin workers was savagely repressed. Ten months later, with defeated Germany facing uprisings throughout the country, soldiers fraternising with workers in Berlin's city centre manned machine guns in trucks flying the red flag of revolution. On 9 November crowds gathered at the Berliner Schloss again, this time to cheer Liebknecht on the balcony proclaiming a socialist republic. However, his rivals, the Social Democrats (SPD), had earlier stolen a march on him by giving their new German Republic the official stamp of a declaration from the Reichstag.

Weimar Republic

Social Democratic **Chancellor Friedrich Ebert** and defence minister **Gustav Noske**, both fiercely anti-Bolshevik, smashed the Spartacist movement with the help of 4 000 right-wing Freikorps(free corps) storm-troopers. Liebknecht and Luxemburg were assassinated on 15 January 1919, four days before the election of a new national assembly. To draw up the republic's constitution at a safe distance from the turbulent capital, delegates moved temporarily to Weimar. On 1 October 1920 a law came into force uniting seven towns (such as Charlottenburg, Spandau and Köpenick), 59 villages and 27 demesnes with Berlin to form the **Gross Berlin**, with a combined population of 3.8 million.

These brutal birth-pains did not augur well for Germany's first attempt at parliamentary democracy. Still embittered by humiliating military defeat, Freikorps storm-troopers staged the **Kapp Putsch** of

March 1920. Their puppet chancellor, provincial bureaucrat Wolfgang Kapp, lasted only five days, but the swastika on their helmets endured as the emblem adopted by the Weimar Republic's destroyers.

Amid the intermittent violence, however, Berlin exploded as Europe's culturally most vibrant, innovative and eccentric capital. Painting, music, theatre and the exciting new art of cinema all thrived, as did sales of whisky and champagne, hashish and cocaine.

The high life – at least for some – was accompanied by ludicrously high inflation for all. Aggravated by growing unemployment, social unrest erupted into bloody street battles between Communist and Nazi agitators. In 1926 from his Munich headquarters, **Adolf Hitler** sent his brilliant propagandist, Joseph Goebbels, to organise Nazi activity in the city of Berlin.

Third Reich and World War

Democracy collapsed as the **Nazis** stepped into the breach left by self-destructive infighting between Social Democrats and Communists. On 30 January 1933 a torch-lit parade of storm-troopers through the Brandenburg Gate celebrated Hitler's appointment as chancellor. Within a month, a fire in the Reichstag building launched the Nazi rule of state-terror. Despite the arrest on the spot of a Dutch Communist, Marinus van der Lubbe (claiming he acted alone), no hard evidence ever proved a concerted Communist plot but it gave Hitler a pretext for wiping out all political opposition. Tracked down by the **Gestapo** secret police of Heinrich Himmler, thousands of Communists and Social Democrats were interned in concentration camps.

Jewish-owned shops and synagogues were smashed, looted and burned on 9 November 1938, an event known as the **Kristallnacht** (The Night of the Broken Glass) because of the shattered glass of a monumental chandelier in the Wertheim department store. It was in a Wannsee villa in January 1942 that a ministerial conference formulated the 'Final Solution of the European Jewish Question'. Of Berlin's 160 564 Jews in 1933, extermination and emigration left only 7 272 in 1945.

With the illusions of 1914 still a bitter memory, Berliners no longer cheered as troops marched off to another war in 1939. This time the fighting came home – the first bombardments occurred in August 1940 as the British retaliated for the air raids on London. In 1944 the American raids took over, day and night, and in April 1945 the Russians began their land attacks. On 30 April, in his bunker below the burning Reich Chancellery on Wilhelmstrasse, Hitler committed suicide.

An enlarged reproduction of Käthe Kollwitz's 'Mother with her Dead Child' stands alone in the Neue Wache, since 1993 an emotionally-laden memorial to the victims of the Third Reich.

The Wall: Peace in a Divided City

At their 1945 **Potsdam Conference**, the Allies placed Berlin under four-power control within Soviet-occupied East Germany, a division which set the stage for the **Cold War**. After the 1946 city-wide elections, the Soviet authorities shielded their eastern sector from any further dangerous democratic experiments. Frustrated by the contagious influence at the heart of East Germany of a capitalist West Berlin, in 1948 the Soviets cut the city's road, rail and waterway links with West Germany. American and British planes broke the blockade by airlifting up to 8 000 tons of food and supplies daily for 11 months. In 1949 East Berlin was declared capital of the German Democratic Republic (GDR).

On 17 June 1953 resentment of poor living conditions and Stalinist repression under the GDR government of **Walter Ulbricht** exploded into violent uprising. Soviet tanks crushed the insurrection, but East Germans continued their protest by fleeing to the west.

Soviet leader **Nikita Khrushchev** directed the East Germans to stop the emigration by closing the East-West Berlin border on 13 August 1961. The formidable **Wall** that grew out of the first barbed-wire and road-block barriers reduced the flow of refugees to a trickle. A few escaped through canals and sewers or secret tunnels but many died in the attempt. Border-crossings were installed for foreigners (notably at the US Army's Checkpoint Charlie, in Friedrichstrasse) and for West Germans. West Berliners could not cross until their former mayor, **Willy Brandt**, had as Chancellor negotiated a thaw in Cold War relations in the 1970s. This was the famous *Ospolitik* (Eastern Policy) of building bridges to the Soviet bloc – later seen by many as the necessary prelude to German unification.

The Wall at the Brandenburg Gate, May 1989, six months before it was pulled down.

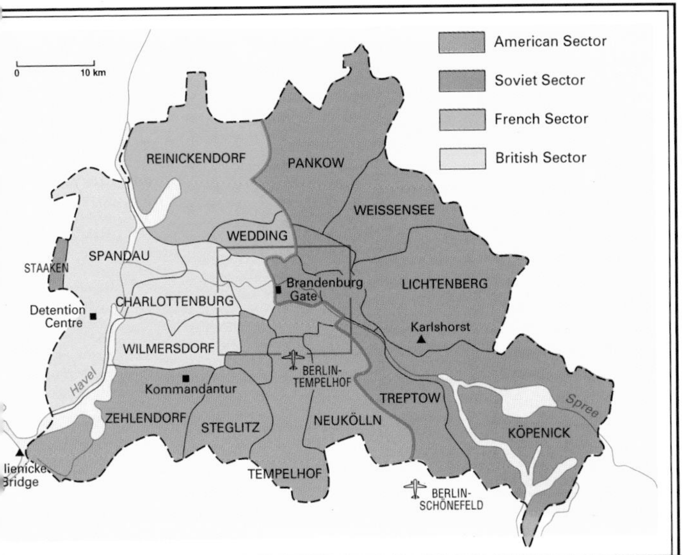

American Sector
Soviet Sector
French Sector
British Sector
0
10 km
REINICKENDORF
PANKOW
WEISSENSEE
WEDDING
SPANDAU
STAAKEN
Brandenburg Gate
LICHTENBERG
CHARLOTTENBURG
Detention Centre
Karlshorst
WILMERSDORF
BERLIN-TEMPELHOF
Havel
Kommandantur
TREPTOW
Spree
ZEHLENDORF
STEGLITZ
NEUKÖLLN
KÖPENICK
TEMPELHOF
BERLIN-SCHÖNEFELD
ACHTUNG!
SIE VERLASSEN JETZT WEST BERLIN

Reunited Capital of a Unified Germany

Ulbricht's successor, **Erich Honecker**, created an artificially bloated East German economy, crippled by endemic corruption and mismanagement. More consumer goods meant only that East Berliners could see on their new colour televisions that the grass was much, much greener on the other side of the Wall. Above all, they became very aware of the personal freedom and cultural diversity of western life as their own dissident writers and artists were being jailed or expelled.

Ecological protests against industrial pollution in Saxony expanded into a national campaign for democracy. The exodus of East German refugees resumed, this time through Hungary, Czechoslovakia and Poland. Reluctant but realistic grave-digger of his own Soviet bloc, **Mikhail Gorbachov** visited East Berlin on 1 October 1989 for the 40th anniversary of the German Democratic Republic, to tell Honecker that Soviet tanks would never again come to its rescue. Honecker resigned on 18 October, and following the resignation of the government of East Germany on 7 November, the Wall opened on **9 November 1989**. Within a year, on 3 October, the national black, red and gold flag rose above the Reichstag to honour German unity, of which Chancellor **Helmut Kohl** was ultimately the canny political architect.

May Day parade.

To simplify day-to-day government, it was voted in 1997 to reorganise the unified city's 23 post-war districts into a more manageable 15.

Exodus to the cheaper rents of the hinterland indicated that the capital's population would not soon return to its 1939 high of 4.3 million.

After the first euphoria, Berliners discovered that the Wall, as much a state of mind as a piece of concrete, had not completely disappeared. Economic and social differences between east and west remained. In municipal elections, the PDS, the more reformist-minded successor party to the Communists, garnered a solid 33 per cent support in the old eastern sector. West and east Berliners rarely visited each other's neighbourhoods. To realise Willy Brandt's eloquent comment: 'Es wächst zusammen, was zusammen gehört,' ('What belongs together, grows together,') may take a little more time.

PEOPLE AND CULTURE

As a result of the generalisations that form popular images of national identity, Germans are not thought of as being particularly witty. Berliners are a forceful exception. In the city's tumultuous history, their humour has been part of their survival kit. Nurtured at the eastern edge rather than at the heart of the country, theirs is a sturdy frontier spirit. Playing a leading role in the city's cultural life, French Huguenots added a little polish, the Jews a warmer, if bitter-sweet, sense of irony. The regimental spirit of the Hohenzollerns and the more recent brutal conformism of Nazis

Political graffiti covers the remaining segments of the Berlin Wall.

and Stalinists never sat well with most Berliners. Their irreverence always made Hitler, Ulbricht and Honecker feel decidedly uncomfortable.

In their role as citizens of a great national capital, Berliners express the appropriate self-confidence, but they have little of the sophistication, even among their taste-makers, that is common in New Yorkers, Londoners or Parisians. Germany's smart set are mostly in Munich, many of them Berlin exiles who could not take the hard years of the Cold War. A token few can be seen in the cafés, bistros and trattorias around Charlottenburg's Savignyplatz.

By a strange quirk of politics, the Cold War renewed the city's youthful spirit that had so captured the world's imagination in the 1920s, only to be destroyed in the Hitler years. To rejuvenate Berlin's ageing population, the West German government offered generous subsidies and exemption from military service to attract a steady flow of young artists and students. This provided the impetus for Berlin's leading role in the 'alternative scene', the enduring German equivalent of underground or counter-culture. Its strongholds, principally in the working-class neighbourhoods of Kreuzberg and, since the fall of the Wall, in Prenzlauer Berg in the east, are threatened now by the 'gentrification' of renovated housing. Angry graffiti are often all that remain of the squatters' once violent resistance to eviction.

Frederick II's extravagant and pompous Rococo New Palace in Potsdam was a statement of the Empire's victorious power.

Architecture

Of Berlin's medieval beginnings, only the much-renovated, originally **late Romanesque** Nikolaikirche (1230) in the old city centre and the nicely preserved **Gothic** ruin of the

Franciscan Klosterkirche (1260) remain.

The royal city took architectural shape in the 17C with the first **Baroque** buildings of **Andreas Schlüter** (1659-1714) and **Johann Arnold Nering**, who worked together on the Zeughaus (Arsenal) and the Hohenzollerns' Berliner Schloss (now destroyed). The arrival of Huguenot Protestants added a French flavour, seen in the Französische Kirche and its twin Deutsche Kirche in the Gendarmenmarkt. Baroque achieved its full flowering under Prussia's 18C absolutist monarchs. To launch Frederick II's classically conceived Forum Fridericianum

in Unter den Linden, Georg von Knobelsdorff (1699-1753) designed the royal opera house (now the Deutsche Staatsoper) and a palace which today houses Humboldt University, while **Christian Unger** built the Alte Bibliothek. Knobelsdorff gave a decorative **Rococo** touch to Frederick II's Schloss Sanssouci and New Palace in Potsdam and to Schloss Charlottenburg, for which **Johann Friedrich Eosander von Göthe** had been chief architect.

The Brandenburg Gate, built by **Carl Gotthard Langhens**, exemplified the Hohenzollern penchant for austere **neo-Classical** monumentality. It was left to the city's greatest architect, **Karl Friedrich Schinkel** (1781-1841), influenced by journeys to Rome and Paris, to add the refinements of eclecticism in his Neue Wache (Royal Guard House), Altes Museum and Schauspielhaus.

Architecturally, united Germany's **Gründerjahre** (Founder Years) meant

Karl Friedrich Schinkel's neo-Classical Schauspielhaus (1820) on the Gendarmenmarkt.

different things to different classes: Mietskasernen (rent-barracks) for the workers, grand villas in Dahlem for the bourgeoisie and, for the Kaiser and his government, the giganticism of the Berliner Dom (Julius Raschdorff) and the Reichstag of Paul Wallot.

The father of 20C **modernism** was **Peter Behrens** (1868-1940) whose functional designs for the AEG electrical works in Wedding and Moabit proved precursors for the great **Bauhaus movement** of the 1920s. **Walter Gropius** (1883-1969) and **Ludwig Mies Van der Rohe** (1886-1969) left examples of their housing design in Zehlendorf and Wedding and, more recently in the Tiergarten, the Neue Nationalgalerie (Mies) and the Bauhaus-Archiv (Gropius). Among the more flamboyant exponents of 1920s **Expressionism** was **Erich Mendelsohn**, who built the cinema that is today the Schaubühne Theatre and the Einstein Tower at Potsdam. **Hans Poelzig** built the imposing Haus des Rundfunks (Radio Building) in 1929, while another Expressionist disciple, **Hans Scharoun** (1893-1972), returned to Berlin after the Second World War to mastermind the Kulturforum and build its Philharmonie and Staatsbibliothek.

Hitler's dislike for Berlin prompted his plan, drawn up by master architect **Albert Speer** (1905-1981), to gut the city of its historic centre and replace it with huge monuments to the glory of National Socialism. The bleak, soulless style for the new capital that would have been known as **'Germania'** can be seen in the Olympic Stadium and the office buildings in Fehrbelliner Platz.

Berlin's return to the status of a world

metropolis is proclaimed by the architects from around the world now working on the areas opened up by the fall of the Wall, notably Renzo Piano's tower on Potsdamer Platz, Jean Nouvel's elegant Galeries Lafayette, Philip Johnson, Pei, and Norman Foster, responsible for the reconstruction of the Reichstag.

Painting and Sculpture

The Hohenzollerns brought the fine arts to Berlin in the 18C. As court painter, Paris-born Huguenot **Antoine Pesne** (1683-1757) decorated the walls and ceilings of Schloss Charlottenburg and Potsdam's Sanssouci with his delicate Rococo landscapes and female portraits. The sculpture expressed the more robust side of the Prussian kings. **Andreas Schlüter** created the equestrian statue of the Great Elector Frederick-William for Schloss Charlottenburg, **Johann Gottfried Schadow** (1764-1850) the Quadriga horses on the Brandenburg Gate, and **Christian Daniel Rauch** (1777-1857) the military heroes on Unter den Linden.

Karl Friedrich Schinkel's 'Garden Scene with the Sphinx in Moonlight' was a set design for Mozart's Magic Flute.

Architect **Karl Friedrich Schinkel** left his mark as a Romantic painter of landscapes and exquisitely executed studies for theatre décors and fanciful Gothic monuments. However, **Caspar David Friedrich** was the most important artist of the romantic genre, exhibiting frequently in the Academy and much admired by the future Frederick William IV.

By the end of the 19C, three Berlin painters were leading the German

Impressionist movement – Max Liebermann (1847-1935), who began as a sombre master of naturalism, Lovis Corinth and Max Slevogt.

The violent emotions depicted in the often garish colours of **Expressionism** exploded in Berlin with the arrival in 1911 of Ernst Ludwig Kirchner (1880-1938) and Karl Schmidt-Rottluff (1884-1976) to join Max Pechstein and Emil Nolde. The climate of freedom in Weimer Germany attracted the **avant-garde** artists from the East and Europe, and people like Kandinsky, Moholy-Nagy, Kokoschka and El Lissitzky were all drawn here.

The craziness of Berlin's 1920s found its first artistic statement in the **Club Dada** movement, led by painter George Grosz and John Heartfield, master of satirical photomontage. Characteristically, Grosz joined with poet Walther Mehring to stage a 'happening' as jockeys in a race between a typewriter and a sewing machine. This absurdist nihilism gave way to the more weighty **Neue Sachlichkeit** (New Objectivity) of which Max Beckmann (1884-1950) and Otto Dix (1891-1969) were major exponents in their uncompromisingly stark, even grim, portraiture.

The wasteland of art under the Nazis was epitomised by the sculpture of **Arno Breker**. His bombastic statues of naked soldiers, workers and athletes representing the Aryan ideal adorned public buildings around Berlin until removed by Allied bombs, or later by embarrassed city officials.

With the city divided, East Berlin artists followed the generally sterile propagandist course of social realism, while western artists renewed older city traditions with the happenings of Wolf Vostell and the **neo-Expressionist** work of Markus Lüpertz and Georg Baselitz. Even the Wall itself made a contribution by inspiring a Berlin version of graffiti art – painted on the western side and preserved in the Mauer Galerie in Mühlenstrasse.

Literature

Berlin's best writers always had a keen eye for the Zeitgeist. Philosopher and dramatist **Gottfried Ephraim Lessing** (1729-1781) developed his ideas in what became the spiritual capital of the **German Enlightenment**. This pioneering feminist, defender of heretics and minorities in general, spent long hours debating with Voltaire at Frederick II's palace in Potsdam. His lifelong friend, Jewish philosopher **Moses Mendelssohn** (1729-1786), saw no difficulty in reconciling religion with his liberal rationalism. His prestige laid the basis for the special place in the city's cultural life of Jewish intellectuals.

In his prose and drama, **Heinrich von Kleist** (1777-1811) was the noblest example of Berlin individualism, an observer at once cool and passionate, defying classification in Germany's Romantic and Classical schools.

Supreme 19C novelist of the newly united Germany, **Theodor Fontane** (1819-1898) masterfully chronicled the foibles of the city's ruling classes in *Effi Briest* and *Die Poggenpuhls*.

The great novel of the metropolis in the 1920s was *Berlin Alexanderplatz*, by **Alfred Döblin** (1878-1957), a searing portrait of the city's proletariat and underworld. In the theatre, **Bertolt Brecht** (1898-1956) took an explicitly Marxist view of society in his

Dreigroschenoper (Threepenny Opera) and *Die heilige Johanna der Schlachthöfe* (St Joan of the Stockyards). While he and director Erwin Piscator staged politically committed revolutionary drama, the seasoned 'magician' **Max Reinhardt** continued to produce mainstream, but no less innovative, spectaculars that proved to be higher-brow theatrical forerunners of Hollywood extravaganzas.

Literature's role in the Third Reich was exemplified by the **book-burning** in front of the university on Unter den Linden. There, on 10 May 1933, students joined Nazi storm-troopers to destroy not only the works of Jewish authors such as Albert Einstein, Sigmund Freud and Stefan Zweig, but also those of 'Aryan' humanists like Thomas Mann and Heinrich Mann, Erich Maria Remarque, and such decadent foreign subversives as H G Wells, André Gide, Marcel Proust, Jack London and Upton Sinclair.

After the war, West Germany's leading novelist, **Günter Grass**, made the city his home and became a close confidant of Willy Brandt. East Berlin attracted leftist exiles like Brecht and novelist Anna Seghers, with such new talents as Uwe Johnson, Christa Wolf and Polish-born Jurek Becker, dramatist **Heiner Müller** and singer-poet **Wolf Biermann** emerging to challenge party-line conformism. True Berliners.

Cinema

A couple of months before the Lumière brothers presented their Cinématographe in Paris in 1895, two Berlin brothers, **Max and Emil Skladanowsky**, put on Europe's first film show. Their Bioscop double-projector proved technically inferior but Berlin's role as a major centre for cinema was established in 1897 with the first feature films of **Oskar Messter**: Frederick the Great playing the flute at Schloss Sanssouci, and an erotic version of Salomé with revolutionary close-ups.

'Nosferatu' (1921), Friedrich Wilhelm Murnau.

Early cinema talent came from Berlin's thriving theatre scene. Master of special lighting effects and handling ensemble acting and crowds on stage, **Max Reinhardt** was less successful in the transition than in his formation of some of the medium's finest talent.

Ernst Lubitsch liked spectacle but his comic taste turned historical costume dramas – *Madame Du Barry* and *Anne Boleyn* – into burlesques. It was his satirical comedies, *The Oyster Princess* and *Kohlhiesel's Daughters*, that won him his ticket to Hollywood in 1923. **Friedrich Wilhelm Murnau** created with the expressionist *Nosferatu* a magically lit masterpiece on the Dracula theme. His psychological drama, *The Last Man*, offered a splendid vehicle for Emil Jannings as a proud hotel doorman relegated to toilet-attendant. He later played the lovelorn teacher in *The Blue Angel*, with which Josef Sternberg launched, in 1930, the international career of Marlene Dietrich.

Berlin cinema combined solid commercialism and high art. *The Cabinet of Dr Caligari* of Robert Wiene was a murder mystery treated with the emotional intensity of German Expressionism. **Fritz Lang** perfected the expressionist form in his portrayal of the city as a hostile and threatening place in his series of films of *Dr Mabuse* (1922). His vision of the conflicts of a non-egalitarian society are explored in *Metropolis* (1925). **Georg Wilhelm Pabst** brought acute psychological analysis and uncompromising realism to his films of war and social comment, and discovered two new stars, Greta Garbo and Louise Brooks in *Loulou.*

Post-war cinema moved away from isolated Berlin, mostly to Munich, but one Berlin talent made a world-wide reputation, **Wim Wenders**, whose *Wings of Desire*, shot two years before the fall of the Wall, captures the city's split personality. **Wolfgang Becker** leads a promisingly free-spirited new generation with a film that evokes superbly post-Wall Berlin: *Life Is a Construction Site.*

'Metropolis' (1925), Fritz Lang.

MUST SEE

Unter den Linden★★

The historic avenue has regained the royal splendour of the **Deutsche Staatsoper★** (National Opera House), embassies, town-palaces and grand hotels.

Brandenburger Tor★★

(Brandenburg Gate)

Dominating the old 'border' between East and West, Berlin's chief landmark was erected in 1791.

Reichstag★

German unification has given the parliament building a new importance, enhanced by Norman Foster's bold glass-and-steel dome.

Gendarmenmarkt★★

Eastern Berlin's most elegant square boasts the Huguenots' **Französischer Dom★**, its twin,

the **Deutscher Dom★**, and Schinkel's **Schauspielhaus★★** (Theatre).

Museumsinsel★★★
(Museums Island)
Eastern Berlin's superb museum complex, with the **Pergamon**'s★★★ monumental Greek and Roman antiquities as its centrepiece.

Schloss Charlottenburg★★
The Hohenzollerns' beautifully restored Baroque and Rococo summer palace is graced with fine paintings by Watteau and Schinkel's **Pavilion★** in the lovely **Schlossgarten★★**.

Ägyptisches Museum★★★
(Egyptian Museum)
A place of pilgrimage which displays the Egyptian treasures, including the **bust★★★** of the beautiful Queen Nefertiti.

Kurfürstendamm★★
The shiny hub of western Berlin remains the city's main shopping street, with chic boutiques and smart open-air cafés providing the best people-watching opportunities in town.

Kulturforum★★★
Berlin's Philharmonic Orchestra, painting, sculpture, decorative arts and the state library come together here in the Tiergarten.

Gemäldegalerie★★★
In the picture gallery's new home in the Tiergarten (due to open in the summer of 1998), works by Rembrandt, Dürer, Vermeer and Caravaggio make this collection of paintings among the best in Europe.

The Bodemuseum on Museumsinsel.

ALONG UNTER DEN LINDEN★★

From the Brandenburg Gate and its elegant 'forecourt', Pariser Platz, the city's celebrated avenue extends over 1km (0.6 mile) to the Schlossbrücke, the Castle Bridge that joined it to the now vanished Berliner Schloss on the island in the Spree. Unter den Linden (NOPYZ) was originally laid out as a bridlepath between the royal castle and the Tiergarten in the shade of the lime, or linden, trees that gave it its name. They are at their most fragrant in June. After Frederick II launched his monumental Forum Fridericianum in the 18C, the avenue became Berlin's most prestigious address. Sharing in the city's building spree, this showcase for Baroque and neo-Classical architecture and harmonious new construction is fast regaining its old

The Kronprinzenpalais (1733) is one of the monumental buildings flanking Unter den Linden.

splendour. New embassies and grand hotels match the spruced-up university, opera house, old library and fine restaurants lodged in town-palaces.

The monumental counterparts of the defunct German Democratic Republic continue east of the gigantic Berliner Dom – parliamentary and party buildings, the Marx-Engels-Forum (beside the quaintly reconstructed medieval Nikolaiviertel), and the Fernsehturm (TV Tower).

Brandenburger Tor** (Brandenburg Gate)
This most emblematic of Berlin monuments (NZ) has had as chequered a history as the city itself. Laden now with symbols of war, peace and national reunification, the only surviving town-gate also served the most mundane of purposes; flanking the central pillared gateway, through which only the royal household could pass, a toll-booth collected customs duties from itinerant merchants and a guard-house watched for deserters from the Prussian Army.

Modelled on Athens' Propylaeum gatehouse to the Parthenon, Carl Gotthard Langhans' neo-Classical structure with its two rows of six Doric columns was completed in 1791 when crowned with the copper **Quadriga**, a four-horse chariot driven by a Winged Victory. Sculptor Johann-Gottfried Schadow conceived her as bringer of peace, carving a Procession of Peace (*Friedenszug*) in sandstone immediately below, but the Prussian kings insisted on celebrating their wars with the gate's other, more belligerent, allegorical friezes.

The Quadriga, so much admired by Napoleon on his entry into the city in 1806

The Brandenburg Gate, symbol of the division of Berlin, has been witness to many of the city's historic struggles but now enjoys more relaxed times.

that he took it back to Paris, was in turn retrieved by his Prussian conqueror, Field Marshal Blücher (*see* p.14). Ever since, the gate has been the focus of revolts for freedom, against the Hohenzollerns in 1848 and against the Stalinist GDR in 1953, of Nazi triumph in 1933, and of the city's division when the Wall went up in 1961 and of its reunification when the Wall was toppled in 1989.

Pariser Platz

The post-Wall wasteland beyond the gate is gradually being revived as the spacious and stately square that originally set the tone for

Unter den Linden's prestige at its west end (NZ), with mansions, embassies and the grandest of hotels. Flanking the Brandenburg Gate, twin sandstone mansions have been resurrected by architect Josef Paul Kleihues to recapture something of their 19C elegance: to the north, **Haus Liebermann**, home of the German Impressionist painter, Max Liebermann, who died there in 1935; and to the south, **Haus Sommer**. Open for business again on the square's south-east corner after total destruction in 1945, the legendary **Adlon Hotel**, founded in 1907, is determined to regain the splendour of the good old days when its guest list included Rockefeller, Einstein, Caruso, Chaplin, Roosevelt (Theodore) and Lawrence of Arabia. Other buildings going up include the **Academie der Künste** (Academy of Fine Arts) next to the Adlon, the French Embassy on the north side, the United States Embassy on the south, and some major banks.

The first part of the avenue east of Pariser Platz is dominated on its south side by the sprawling **Russian Embassy**, constructed in classical Stalinist style in 1953, the year of the dictator's death.

Deutsche Staatsbibliothek
(National Library)

Unter den Linden's royal monuments begin with this formidable neo-Baroque edifice, completed in characteristic massive format for Kaiser William II in 1914, to house the royal Prussian library that had outgrown Frederick II's more graceful 18C **Alte Bibliothek**★ (1775-1781) across the street (*see below*). It is said to house over 6 million books, manuscripts, musical scores, prints and maps.

Denkmal Friedrichs II
(Frederick II Monument)
In the centre of the avenue (OZ), the bronze equestrian statue by Christian Daniel Rauch of the Hohenzollerns' most cultivated king was unveiled here in 1851. Mounted on a pedestal of sculpted reliefs portraying the monarch's soldiers and scholars, it was, in its new historical realism, the artistically most successful of a long series of 19C Prussian monuments serving the nationalist cause. The statue sat out the Second World War in the king's Schloss Sanssouci (*see* p.93) in Potsdam and did not return here till the GDR overcame its anti-monarchist resistance in 1981.

The Frederick II Monument was one of the first of a series of increasingly large and extravagant monuments in the city.

Forum Fridericianum★ (Bebelplatz)
The statue of Frederick II stands beside the edifices which, under his impetus, put an elegant stamp on the royal avenue. Projecting from the east side of Bebelplatz is the **Deutsche Staatsoper★** (National Opera House, *see* p.107), the 1743 design of Georg von Knobelsdorff. With a sober Classical exterior and a more decorative Rococo interior, it was an appropriate founding edifice for the music-loving monarch's forum. Opposite is the **Alte Bibliothek★**, now part of Humboldt University and nicknamed by Berliners 'the Kommode' (chest of drawers). Its curving façade echoes the plans for Vienna's Hofburg Palace. Off to one

The Alte Bibliothek was said to contain some 160 000 books in the 18C.

corner of the square, south of the opera house, is Knobelsdorff's **St Hedwigs Kathedrale**. Frederick II had it built for the Roman Catholic community that came to Berlin after his conquest of Silesia.

Humboldt-Universität
(Humboldt University)

Originally a royal palace designed by Knobelsdorff for Frederick II and finally given to the king's brother, Prince Henry, it became the home of Berlin's first university in 1810 under the leadership of Prussian statesman and philologist **Wilhelm von Humboldt** (*see* p.15). Its first rector was philosopher Johann Gottlieb Fichte, champion of the German national ideal. Teachers and scholars included Hegel, Schopenhauer, the brothers Grimm, Einstein and Max Planck. Bored by his classes, poet Heinrich Heine looked out longingly at the opera house across the street. Today, the university (OY) numbers over 22 000 students, some of them paying for their studies by selling, with difficulty, the works of former alumnus Karl Marx at the entrance.

Exhibits in the Deutsches Historisches Museum.

Neue Wache

Next to the university, the Doric-porticoed **Prussian Army guard-house** (1818) was Karl Friedrich Schinkel's first neo-Classical building for Berlin and now shelters a controversial national memorial, **Gedenkstätte der Bundesrepublik** (*see* p.19). The monument chosen by Chancellor Helmut Kohl – Käthe Kollwitz's bronze sculpture of a mother mourning her dead son – made no distinction between the victims of Nazism and perpetrators in the German army until public outcry insisted on explanatory plaques. Others objected, on aesthetic grounds, to the ponderous enlarged version of what was a poignant miniature of 40cm (16 inches) to four times its original size.

Zeughaus★★

The splendid edifice (PY) built at the end of the 17C as an arsenal for the Prussian Army now houses the **Deutsches Historisches Museum★★** (German History Museum), due to close for renovation at the end of 1998. Its rich collections trace the nation's extraordinary history with paintings, photographs, documentaries and feature films from the silent and modern eras. The building, a Baroque masterpiece, included among its architects Andreas Schlüter, who sculpted the magnificent series of **warrior death-masks★** in the courtyard that bears his name. Here the Chinese-American architect I M Pei has designed a new glassed-over space to shelter the museum's special exhibitions.

Opernpalais

The 18C Baroque residence of Prussian princesses – originally the Prinzessinnen-palais – has been charmingly reconstructed to house a popular open-air café, two elegant restaurants and a bar. It is linked by a roofed bridge to the neighbouring **Kronprinzenpalais**★ (Crown Princes' Palace), built for the future Frederick II in 1733 and used now as a German government residence. In the palace grounds are 19C military statues, by Christian Daniel Rauch, of the German generals who defeated Napoleon – Blücher, with drawn sabre and his foot on a broken cannon, flanked by Yorck and Gneisenau.

Fischerinsel★ (Fishermen's Island)

The district at the southern end of the island was the site of one of Berlin's earliest settlements, now replaced by modern housing blocks. At the northern end is the **Museumsinsel**★★★ (Museums Island) (OPY), the monumental museum complex including the famous Pergamonmuseum, Bodemuseum and Altes Museum (*see* p.80). The Hohenzollern kings made their home in the middle of the island.

Schinkel's **Schlossbrücke**★ (Castle Bridge, 1824), adorned with some fine bronze reliefs of seahorses, dolphins and tritons as well as more military statuary, links Unter den Linden to the vast **Schlossplatz** (PYZ). Here, after clearing away most of the bombed royal castle as an offensive symbol of imperialism, the East German Communists staged parades of workers, soldiers and tanks to celebrate May Day and other great ideological anniversaries. The royal castle was replaced by the GDR's bronze glass, steel and white marble **Palast der Republik** (Palace of the Republic). Designed in deliberate contrast to the castle as a 'house of the people', it originally combined the East German

The splendid Castle Bridge spanning the Spree is decorated with a series of fine statues and bronze reliefs.

parliament with restaurants, discothèques and a bowling alley, but now it, too, faces destruction, because of its dangerous asbestos content. The GDR's **Staatsrat** (State Council) building on the south side of the square incorporates the only surviving remnant of the royal castle – the Baroque balcony from which Karl Liebknecht proclaimed a socialist republic in 1918, waving a red blanket as a flag. In the south-east corner is the **Stadtbibliothek** (Town Library), housed in part in Berlin's only surviving Renaissance building, the gabled **Ribbeckhaus** (Ribbeck House) of 1629.

Berliner Dom★ (Berlin Cathedral)

The various churches built since the 15C on this site (PY), north of Schlossplatz, have always expressed the political will of their monarch. The huge neo-Baroque edifice erected in 1905 for Kaiser William II served as the court church and mausoleum for the Hohenzollerns. Its enormous dome surrounded by four towers reflects his wish to give German Protestantism an awesome counterpart to St Peter's in Rome.

In the bright and colourful **interior★★**, holding a congregation of over 2 000, notice the finely carved **wooden lectern** by Andreas Schlüter, and the monumental **iron candelabras** designed by the multi-talented Schinkel. Six Hohenzollern **sarcophagi** and **tomb monuments** are in the main church; another 97 members of the dynasty are buried in the **Hohenzollern crypt** (Gruft).

Marx-Engels-Forum

The past pomp of East German Communism is timidly commemorated on this green square with **bronze statues** of Karl Marx and Friedrich Engels.

Below left: The distinctive Red Town Hall and Neptune Fountain.

The neo-Baroque Berliner Dom contrasts with the modern Palast der Republik.

Rotes Rathaus★ (Red Town Hall)
Seat of the Berlin Senate, this handsome Red Town Hall – so named for its red brick, rather than for any ideological reason – stands on the site of the city's first 13C town hall (PY). It was designed in 1869 by Hermann Friedrich Waesemann in Tuscan neo-Romanesque style. Above the ground floor is a **terracotta frieze** of 36 panels depicting the great events in Berlin's history.

Nikolaiviertel★

Between the town hall, the Spree and the Mühlendamm embankment is a reconstruction of the city's medieval neighbourhood (PQYZ), popular now for its charming restaurants and cafés. It takes its name from the parish church, the twin-steepled Gothic **Nikolaikirche★**, originally built in 1230 and today exhibiting collections of the **Märkisches Museum** (Brandenburg March Museum) devoted to folklore and the city's history. Also serving as museums are two graceful old houses – the

St George and the Dragon go into battle in the Nikolaiviertel, with the twin spires of the Nikolaikirche beyond.

Opposite top: The original Ephraim Palace was built for Frederick II's court jeweller; the building we see today is a reconstruction.

Opposite bottom: The 356m (1 200ft) Television Tower dwarfs its neighbour, the 13C Marienkirche.

Baroque and Rococo **Ephraim Palais**★ (originally built in 1766 but destroyed in 1935 and replaced with a copy), once home of Frederick II's banker and jeweller, Nathan Veitel Ephraim; and the **Knoblauchhaus**★, a bourgeois mansion with a Classical façade of 1800.

Fernsehturm★ (Television Tower)

Like so many of these overgrown TV antennae, the best thing about the tower is the **view**★★★ you get from it (*see* p.7). Built as East Berlin's self-congratulatory monument in 1969 to dwarf West Berlin's 'mini-Eiffel Tower', the 1920s Funkturm (QY) in Charlottenburg, it measures 365m (1 200ft) to the highest point. A revolving observation deck and café are in the seven-storey sphere housing the offices of Deutsches Telekom.

Marienkirche

The belfry of the 13C Gothic parish church (PY) makes a delicate contrast to the TV Tower. Inside are a 15C carved **wooden altar** and **Totentanz** (Dance of Death) frieze in the north aisle, and a monumental marble **pulpit**★ (1703) by Andreas Schlüter.

Alexanderplatz*

Site of Berlin's first subway station in 1913, the city's busiest square in the 1920s achieved international renown with **Alfred Döblin's** great proletarian novel *Berlin Alexanderplatz*. The vast open space of 'Alex' (QY) awaits renovation to regain its old momentum with a project of Manhattan-style skyscrapers. Today, its chief monuments are Peter Behrens' architectural landmarks, **Berolina** and **Alexanderhaus**, built in 1930 for shops, restaurants and offices, the **universal clock 'Urania'** and a couple of 1960s hotel and department-store towers. Architecture buffs interested in a relic of the bleak Stalinist style can take a quick side-trip east along **Karl-Marx-Allee** (formerly Stalin Allee).

The 'Fountain of Friendship of the Nations', by artist W Womacka, stands in the centre of Alexanderplatz.

AROUND KURFÜRSTENDAMM**

Long before the Wall divided the city in two, the 'Prince Elector's Embankment', popularly known just as the Ku'damm (BU), embodied the smarter western half of Berlin's social life. Ever since the German occupation of Paris in the Franco-Prussian War of 1870-1871, Bismarck had wanted the avenue to match the Champs-Élysées. The bourgeoisie's town houses were joined by theatres, fine restaurants and shops, and by the 1920s the avenue at the heart of the Neuer Westen (New West), already both elegant and garish, had successfully challenged the supremacy of Unter den Linden and Friedrichstrasse. The Nazis hated its cosmopolitan polish; its shop-windows, café terraces and big cinemas made it in the

Cold War years the natural centrepiece of capitalism's showcase for the Western way of life. When the Wall was breached, East Berliners headed first for the bright lights of the Ku'damm.

KaDeWe*

The spirit of the Ku'damm in fact begins south-west of the avenue in **Tauentzienstrasse**, at this grandest of German department stores, a monument in its own right more formally known by its full name, **Kaufhaus des Westens** (Department Store of the West), a name it has borne since 1907. If the newly 'liberated' East Berliners went on the night of 9 November to the Ku'damm, the next morning they stormed KaDeWe. 'If it's not here,' says the seasoned shopper, 'it's not in Berlin.' Gourmets, not an especially spoiled breed in Berlin, find solace among the extravagant displays of the food halls.

KaDeWe, Europe's largest department store, welcomes some 80 000 shoppers every day.

Europa-Center

At the entrance to the Ku'damm in Breitscheidplatz, this hotel, cinema and shopping complex was conceived as another consumer symbol of 1960s capitalism. In the Cold War game, of which the Fernsehturm in Alexanderplatz was a Communist example, the 22-storey tower was topped by a Mercedes-Benz star erected quite deliberately to shine into East Berlin. The square's modern granite **Weltkugelbrunnen** (Fountain of the World) is a popular meeting place for clowns, skateboarders and tired tourists.

Kaiser-Wilhelm-Gedächtniskirche★
(Kaiser Wilhelm Memorial Church)
In a city so full of symbols, few are as eloquent as this ruin of Germany's imperial past. The **spire** of the church, built in honour of Kaiser William I, was decapitated by Second World War bombs and is flanked now by a new octagonal church and hexagonal belltower and a chapel to evoke the city's rebirth. In the remains of the neo-Romanesque church (1895) is a **hall** commemorating with friezes and carved reliefs the Hohenzollern dynasty, from the 15C Prince-Elector Frederick I to the last

With its spire truncated in the Second World War, the Kaiser Wilhelm Memorial Church makes one of Berlin's more poignant landmarks.

crown prince, another William, who died in 1951. **Stained glass** from Chartres, France, lends dignity to the modern edifices (1963), but the symbolic aspirations of church, past and present, are given a characteristically wry twist by the Berliners' nicknames for them: 'broken tooth' for the old steeple and 'lipstick' and 'powder compact' for the latter-day additions.

Kurfürstendamm★★

The Ku'damm (BU) began life, like Unter den Linden, as a royal bridlepath, in this case to the Hohenzollerns' hunting lodge in the Grunewald. Bismarck wanted to extend the avenue all the way to the forest but his republican successors made do with the more prosaic Halensee railway station, 3.5km (just over 2 miles) from the Gedächtniskirche.

Spend an hour or two watching the world pass by at Café Kranzler, a traditional meeting place for the Berliner bourgoisie.

A stroll along the avenue begins – or ends – at **Café Kranzler**, the café terrace at the corner of Joachimsthalerstrasse, a great place for people-watching. Whereas the original Kranzler in Unter den Linden was a meeting place for radicals plotting the 1848 revolution, the biggest threat posed by its successor is high cholesterol from the delicious pastries. The café faces a threat of its own, being dwarfed by a gigantic new glass office block by Helmut Jahn.

The Chicago architect's critically better-received **Ku'70** (at the other end of the avenue on the corner of Lewishamstrasse) is an imaginative *tour de force*, a slender curving glass tower wedged into a space only 2.5m (barely 8ft) wide at ground level. Across the avenue further west is what has long been the city's most adventurous theatre, the **Schaubühne**★, its bold façade curving back on Lehniner Platz. Its modern restoration preserves Erich Mendelsohn's innovative 1920s Woga complex, originally housing a cinema, cabaret, apartments, a hotel and shops.

Among the few surviving examples of bourgeois apartment-houses from the avenue's grand era around the end of the 19C are No 15, with its neo-Baroque façade; No 35, brick with terracotta ornament; No 37, with its Jugendstil (art nouveau) balconies and bay windows; and the massive corner house at Leibnizstrasse, No 59, where the apartments had up to 11 huge rooms before being divided up into more manageable modern units.

Fasanenstrasse★

Of the elegant cross-streets that are an integral part of the Ku'damm area, this is one of the finest, known particularly for luxury boutiques and restaurants. Besides its gleaming marble-and-glass shopping galleries set in secluded courtyards, it boasts some of the neighbourhood's most imposing villas. South of the Ku'damm, the Wintergarten-Ensemble, Nos 23-27, groups four houses built from 1871 to 1892 that include the **Galerie Pels-Leuden**, the **Käthe-Kollwitz Museum**★ (of the militant sculptor's life and work) and the **Literaturhaus** at No 23, with its bookshop and garden-restaurant frequented by writers and publishers. On the north-west corner is the Ku'damm's most prestigious hotel and restaurant, the **Kempinski**, well worth at least a visit to the opulent bar.

Further north on the opposite side, set back in a garden at No 79, is the **Jüdisches Gemeindehaus** (Jewish Community Centre). This modern building retains over its main entrance the domed porch of the 1911 synagogue burned down by the Nazis on the fateful Kristallnacht (*see* p.19) – one of 34 Berlin synagogues to be destroyed that night.

Savignyplatz*

Take Grolmannstrasse north, beyond the elevated S-Bahn railway, to this fashionable square where Berlin's writers, artists and show-business people are drawn by the galleries, bookshops, cafés and the Italian, French or refined German cuisine. The house at No 5 was the last home of satirical painter George Grosz, who died there in 1959 after his return from exile in the US and one last momentous bar-crawl around the square that had provided so much subject matter in the 1920s.

The arches under the S-Bahn railway accommodate shops in the fashionable Savignyplatz area.

Bahnhof Zoologischer Garten (Zoo Station)

What was before reunification West Berlin's most important railway station has remained a focus for the seedy, but vibrant, marginal underside of city life, an essential 'other face' of the Ku'damm neighbourhood. However, it has cleaned up its act in the main entrance hall's bright and cheerful shopping centre – open late and on Sundays: the stand selling hot, fresh pretzels outside is an institution.

Zoologischer Garten*** (Zoo)
Zoo-lovers can make their way through the fanciful pagoda-arched Elephant Gate in Budapester Strasse (BU) to one of Europe's richest collections of exotic animals – giant pandas from China, elephants from both India and Africa, crocodiles and Indian rhinoceros, to name but a few.

The elephants welcome visitors to the Zoological Gardens.

TIERGARTEN**

Immediately adjoining the western city centre, the neighbourhood takes its name from the 'Animal Garden' (NZ) that was once a royal hunting forest for wild boar and deer, and is now an agreeable public park for picnicking – popular for Turkish barbecues – boating and rock concerts. In and around it are august parliamentary and government buildings, embassies, the modern Kulturforum centre for music and the fine arts, flea markets and the mushrooming construction in Potsdamer Platz.

The park's trees have not had an easy time of it. Frederick II chopped down the original forest to create a formal French garden for his brother, August Ferdinand, and new groves planted in the 19C for an English-style landscaped park were again felled – for fuel in the bitter winters following the Second World War. Today's trees date from the 1950s, some of them planted by the British in the **Englischer Garten*** (English Garden) on the north side of the park.

Houseboats provide tranquil homes on the Landwehrkanal, which cuts through the southern side of the Tiergarten.

Reichstag★

At the Tiergarten's east end the **Reichstag★** (Parliament) (NY), completed in 1894, has had as turbulent a career as German democracy itself. Hostile to the very thought of a parliament, Kaiser William II worried that Paul Wallot's overpowering neo-Classical design would dwarf the royal castle, and was comforted only when an imperial crown was set on top of the original dome. In the architrave above the six-columned western portico, the dedication DEM DEUTSCHEN VOLKE (To The German People), long-resisted by the Kaiser, was added in 1916 when he was too preoccupied by the First World War to maintain his opposition. The assembly was gutted by the 1933 fire that gave Hitler his pretext to end all parliamentary representation for the German people, and the dome, with its imperial crown, was for safety's sake removed by explosives in the Second World

The Reichstag has had a chequered history but the future looks hopeful, with plans currently in progress to restore it as the seat of the German parliament.

War. Until Berlin was reunified, the Reichstag was dismissed as a useless pile. It regained popular favour only after Bulgarian conceptual artist Christo and his wife wrapped the whole building in fabric in 1995, attracting 5 million visitors (though not Chancellor Helmut Kohl, who hated the idea, and only reluctantly agreed to it becoming once again the home of the German Bundestag). Now it is to have a new glass dome designed by British architect Norman Foster, with a ramp spiralling up inside it to give parliamentarians a loftier view of the world.

Spreebogen

The area of the 'meander of the Spree River' extending north and west of the Reichstag is being transformed into a new government district, designed by Berlin architects Axel Schultes and Charlotte Franck as a symbolic unifying link between the old West Berlin neighbourhood of Moabit and East Berlin's Mitte. Planned for completion between 1999 and 2002, it will include the **Bundeskanzleramt** (Federal Chancellor's Office), the **Bundesrat** (Federal Council, Germany's upper chamber), parliamentary office buildings and a spectacular new national and international railway station, the **Lehrter Bahnhof**.

Haus der Kulturen der Welt*

The low-slung, curved building, known until 1987 as the Kongresshalle, and popularly to Berliners as 'the pregnant oyster' ('die schwangere Auster'), now stages shows and exhibitions of the 160 nations represented on Berlin's multi-cultural scene. In front is a 68-bell **carillon tower**, set to chime at noon and 6pm.

Schloss und Park Bellevue
Built in 1785 for Frederick II's younger brother August Ferdinand, the official residence of the German president is a handsome neo-Classical palace with a splendid ballroom designed by Carl Gotthard Langhans, architect of the Brandenburg Gate. The attractive gardens were laid out after the Second World War by Britain's Shropshire Horticultural Society.

Severely damaged during the war, Schloss Bellevue has been restored to its former splendour.

Hansaviertel
This smart residential neighbourhood, between the palace and the Tiergarten S-Bahn station, grew in its present form out of Interbau's 1957 international design competition as a conscious counterpart to the showpiece Stalinist architecture going up on what is now Karl-Marx Allee. Among the best, each with the architect's name on a plaque, are apartment-houses by Bauhaus master Walter Gropius (Händelallee 3-9), Finland's Alvar Aalto (Klopstockstrasse 30 and 32) and Brazil's Oscar Niemeyer (Altonaer Strasse 4-14).

Siegessäule (Victory Column)
In the middle of the Grosser Stern traffic circle, the monument soaring from the

heart of the Tiergarten Park celebrates Prussian militarism at its height. Designed to commemorate triumph over Denmark in 1864, it was completed in 1873, by which time further successes – over Austria in 1866 and France in 1871 – could be added to the glory of Friedrich Drake's gilded Winged Victory at the top. Its bronze, and that of reliefs depicting the battles and military parades, came from melted-down cannons and other victory spoils. The **view★★** from the top rewards the effort of climbing 285 stairs. On the north side of the traffic circle are monuments to the wars' heroes: Chancellor Bismarck, Field Marshal Moltke and War Minister Roon.

The 60m (197ft) high Victory Column, erected to commemorate Prussia's great military conquests, is topped with Drake's gilded Winged Victory.

Strasse des 17 Juni

Named after the date of the 1953 workers' uprising in East Berlin, the great avenue (BCU) leading west to Charlottenburg and east to the Brandenburg Gate was once used for military parades by the Western Allies. The 1946 **Sowjetisches Ehrenmal** (Soviet War Memorial) remains, as does Berlin's biggest flea market, held every weekend.

Diplomatenviertel (Embassy Row)

It was in the Hitler years that the southern edge of the park became Embassy Row as part of Nazi architect Albert Speer's grandiose project for the new capital, Germania. Appropriately enough, it was

The view from the Victory Column, looking along Strasse des 17 Juni towards the Tiergarten.

Germany's Axis allies whose bombastic buildings survive to recall the spirit of the times: the Italian Embassy at Tiergartenstrasse 21a and the nearby Japanese Embassy at No 24.

Kulturforum★★★ (Cultural Forum)
The buildings at the south-east corner of the Tiergarten celebrate Berlin's attachment to classical music, sculpture and painting, the decorative arts and literature, but not least of all to architecture itself. After the combined devastations of Albert Speer's urban planning and the bombs of the Second World War, Hans Scharoun

The 20C steel and glass of the New National Gallery contrasts with the neo-Romanesque St-Matthäus-Kirche.

masterminded this centrepiece of western Berlin's architectural renewal. Though it is not strictly part of Scharoun's project, the forum also embraces the stark black steel and glass **Neue Nationalgalerie**★★ (New National Gallery, *see* p.85) of late-19C and 20C art, designed by Mies van der Rohe and completed in 1968, a year before his death. Its purity of line and form epitomise the Bauhaus master's maxim that 'less is more'.

Scharoun's own more flamboyant taste for free-form structures is expressed in his sprawling **Staatsbibliothek**★ (State Library), Potsdamer Strasse 33, and the more compact but equally fanciful **Philharmonie★★★** concert hall, at Matthäikirchestrasse 1. Here, the ochre-and-gold roof and walls are draped like a makeshift tent over an auditorium that gives the great Berlin Philharmonic Orchestra optimal acoustics and the audience stunning sightlines.

The Philharmonie concert hall is not only a remarkable piece of architecture, but has excellent acoustics and seats an audience of 2 200.

Besides the brand new **Gemäldegalerie★★★** (*see* p.84), the forum includes the **Musikinstrumenten-Museum★** (Musical Instruments Museum), the **Kammermusiksaal** (Chamber Music Hall) with its multiple white façades, and the ponderous red-brick and white-marble **Kunstgewerbemuseum★★** (Decorative Arts Museum), housing a magnificent collection of porcelain and jewellery (notably the 12C **Guelph Treasure★★★** 'Welfenschatz'), textiles and furniture, including modern designs of the 20C.

St-Matthäus-Kirche

Behind the Neue Nationalgalerie, left in poignant isolation by Hitler's initial ground-clearance for his planned Germania city-of-the-future, this graceful neo-Romanesque church (1846) by Schinkel's pupil, Friedrich-August Stüler, makes its own wry comment on the modern and avant-garde forms around it.

Potsdamer Platz

In the decade since reunification, Europe's biggest construction project has been the transformation of the vast square back into a major downtown area to rival Kurfürstendamm and Unter den Linden. As the site of Berlin's first railway station in

1838, Potsdamer Platz grew from a sleepy crossroads into a bustling traffic hub for the whole city. Massive bombardment in 1944 and the building of the Wall left a wasteland covering 48 hectares (120 acres). Before the Wall went up, its strategic location at the junction of the American, British and Soviet sectors did at least create a thriving black market.

Life is returning, with luxury hotels, shops, apartment buildings and an entertainment complex around the monumental corporate headquarters for Daimler-Benz and Sony. For the Japanese company, Jahn's fibre-glass pyramid will house the **Deutsche Kinemathek** (German Film Library) and **Deutsche Mediathek** (Multimedia Reference Library). In the centre of the site is the bright red Info Box, mounted on stilts to give the public a superb view of the construction and keep them informed of its

The vast building site of Potsdamer Platz has become a tourist attraction in its own right, with a visitor centre and viewing platform.

progress, with audio-visual aids, brochures and books. Nearby, just as a reminder of the way things were, is a piece of the Berlin Wall, complete with fading graffiti.

KREUZBERG**

Principal centre of Berlin's celebrated 'alternative' culture, the neighbourhood extending south-east of Potsdamer Platz (CU) has undergone major changes since reunification. As long as the Wall hemmed it in, Kreuzberg was a haven for artists and drop-outs of the post-1968 social revolution, largely ignored by the Berlin establishment. They squatted in derelict houses as free-living co-operatives, in relative harmony with the influx of immigrant workers who made Kreuzberg the largest Turkish community outside Turkey itself. In the 1990s the bourgeoisie rediscovered the borough's charms, renovated the better 19C houses

Kreuzberg is still a colourful and somewhat unconventional district.

and raised rents. Many Turks have prospered, and the neighbourhood has acquired a tidier but still bustling appeal.

Oranienstrasse*

The borough's liveliest thoroughfare, particularly at night, sustains a colourful mix of 'alternative' bars, health-food and junk shops, with Turkish groceries and restaurants.

Landwehrkanal**

Several Jugendstil (art nouveau) houses have been beautifully restored on the north bank: Fränkel- and Paul-Lincke-Ufer, with fashionable cafés and boutiques on the ground floor and grand balconied apartments above. On the south bank, Maybachufer, the spices, fish, fruits and fabrics of the **Turkish Market**** on Tuesday and Friday afternoons add an eastern Mediterranean bazaar atmosphere (*see* p.122).

Around Viktoriapark*

The little hill that gives Kreuzberg its name rises above the park, with a waterfall and the neo-Gothic **Kriegsdenkmal** (National Monument), designed by Karl Friedrich Schinkel to commemorate Germany's victories over Napoleon. There is a fine **view**** from the top of the hill. Walk north to Grossbeerenstrasse 56, the entrance to the borough's finest residential quarter, **Riehmers Hofgarten***, where lofty apartments in neo-Renaissance and Classical style are set in tranquil gardens.

To the north-west is the **Deutsches Technik Museum**** (Transport and Technology Museum), which has sections covering radio and television, computer science, railways, the textile industry and inland navigation.

FRIEDRICHSTRASSE★ TO PRENZLAUER BERG★★

During the 1920s, when Unter den Linden epitomised pomp and circumstance, the Friedrichstrasse area (OXYZ) made its mark as a boisterous centre of cafés and theatres. Reconstruction since 1989 has brought the street and its environs a new sophistication, with some of the city's smartest new shops, luxury hotels, offices and apartment buildings. Like Potsdamer Platz, it had suffered from broad tracts of no-man's-land left by the Wall. Friedrichstrasse's Checkpoint Charlie became world-famous as the US Army's crossing point for non-Germans – and confrontation between American and Soviet tanks.

Further north, divided German families met at the railway station, Bahnhof Friedrichstrasse, earning it the nickname of Tränenpalast (Palace of Tears) (UY). East of Friedrichstrasse are the lively working-class and former Jewish neighbourhoods of Oranienburger Strasse and Prenzlauer Berg, both popular with artists of Berlin's 'alternative' culture.

Many of the ingenious means of escaping to the West are displayed in the Haus am Checkpoint Charlie, once the border crossing for foreigners.

Checkpoint Charlie

Between Koch- and Zimmerstrasse, two buildings mark the past and present of this former East-West Berlin border crossing. Housed in the old Café Kölln, from which foreign correspondents phoned in their news from the front, the little **Haus am Checkpoint Charlie** is a museum devoted to a painstaking, often tendentious, documentation of the Wall's daily tragedies and the Cold War in general. The other building, in fact an ambitious complex of office buildings, marks the continuing US commitment to the site, with the American Business Center designed by New York architects, Philip Johnson and David Childs.

Quartier Schützenstrasse

Just off Friedrichstrasse, a few steps north-east of Checkpoint Charlie, this colourful block of shops, offices and apartments is one of the more delightful innovations in Berlin's latter-day reconstruction. Milan architect Aldo Rossi has created a collage of brightly painted **façades**, drawing on German 19C forms and 'quotations' from Italian Renaissance masters Andrea Sangallo and Michelangelo, all concealing traditional Berlin *Hinterhöfe* (rear courtyards).

Gendarmenmarkt**

In contrast to the neighbourhood's relentless modernism is the gentle harmony of this 18C square (OZ) commissioned by King Frederick I for the Baroque church he offered the French Huguenots, the **Französischer Dom*** (1701), and its twin counterpart for German Protestants, the **Deutscher Dom*** (1708). Recently reconstructed, both are modelled on a

Charenton church, with domes added in the 1780s. The French church houses the **Hugenottenmuseum** (Huguenot Museum) and in the German church is the Bundestag's permanent exhibition, **Fragen an die deutsche Geschichte** (German History in Question).

On the west side of the square is Karl Friedrich Schinkel's masterly neo-Classical **Schauspielhaus**★★ (Theatre, *see* p.26), built in 1820, with Reinhold Begas' white marble **statue of Schiller**. The square owes its military name to a regiment of guards garrisoned here by the Sergeant King, Frederick-William I.

Schiller's statue stands on the Gendarmenmarkt, with the Französischer Dom beyond, mirroring the Deutscher Dom across the square.

Friedrichstrasse★

The street's new splendour is highlighted by a series of luxurious buildings, starting underground at Nos 71-74 with Friedrichstadtpassagen, the opulent shopping galleries designed by Henry Cobb. At the intersection with Französische Strasse is Jean Nouvel's spectacular curving **Galeries Lafayette building**★ (No 207) (OZ), diagonally across from the hotel, offices and restaurants of Josef Paul Kleihues' Hofgarten am Gendarmenmarkt (No 208, backing onto the 18C square).

The old theatre district begins north of Bahnhof Friedrichstrasse with the **Metropol**, home of operettas and musical comedies. Bertolt Brecht's **Berliner Ensemble** is across

The fashionable shopping galleries of Friedrichstadt-passagen, in Friedrichstrasse, the main shopping street of the Mitte district.

the Spree River on Schiffbauerdamm. The **Deutsches Theater**, founded by Max Reinhardt in the Schumannstrasse, is still going strong, and the grand variety hall of **Friedrichstadtpalast** has been given a brassy new lease on life at Friedrichstrasse 107.

Oranienburger Strasse★★

This busy shopping street (OX) was the main thoroughfare of the **Scheunenviertel** (Barn District), created in the 17C to keep dangerous inflammable grain storehouses away from the city centre. First stop for poor Jewish refugees from Russia and Poland, it became in the 1920s a notorious district for seedy nightclubs, prostitutes and criminals. It still has a bouncing nightlife and the houses' rear courtyards have been renovated with shops, art galleries, off-beat cafés and restaurants. At No 54, **Tacheles**, a Yiddish word roughly meaning 'straight talking', is a highly active artists' co-operative presently installed in the ruin of an abandoned shopping gallery. Further east, the 19C **Ehemaliges Postfuhramt und Haupttelegraphenamt*** (former Postal Coach Office), at No 35 on the corner of Tucholskystrasse, is a handsome glazed brick and terracotta neo-Renaissance building.

The recently reconstructed New Synagogue was originally built to hold a congregation of 3 000.

Dominating the street at No 30 are the gleaming gilded and glass Moorish-inspired domes of the **Neue Synagoge** (New Synagogue) (OX). Consecrated in 1866, Germany's finest synagogue was saved from the Kristallnacht fires of 1938 (*see* p.19) by a courageous local policeman – only to fall victim to an Allied bomb in 1943. With a small room now reserved for religious services, the major part of the beautifully restored interior is given over to the **Centrum Judaicum** and its exhibition of the community's history.

Nearby, a few steps north in Grosse Hamburger Strasse, is the gravestone of **Moses Mendelssohn** (1729-1786), illustrious philosopher, in what was Berlin's first **Jewish cemetery** until it was razed by the Nazis.

Hackesche Höfe*

Behind tastefully restored Jugendstil (art nouveau) façades of 1907, the seven courtyards (Höfe) of its name extend from

Jugendstil façades from the turn of the century have been restored at Hackesche Höfe.

Rosenthaler back to **Sophienstrasse★** (PX). They form a charming self-contained neighbourhood of apartments, art galleries, boutiques, cafés, avant-garde theatre and cinema.

Prenzlauer Berg★★

The bustling **Schönhauser Allee** (QX 270) shopping street is the main thoroughfare of eastern Berlin's most characterful working-class neighbourhood. At No 23, the **Jüdischer Friedhof★** (Jewish Cemetery) is the last resting place of composer Giacomo Meyerbeer, publisher Leopold Ullstein and

Café-life in Kollwitzplatz, popular haunt of writers and artists.

painter Max Liebermann. The cafés and bars in **Kollwitzplatz★** are a favourite meeting place for artists and writers from all over Berlin. Always a focus of resistance to established authority, Prenzlauer Berg was the last holdout against the Nazis, flying the red flag from the **Wasserturm** (water tower) on Wörtherstrasse until the Gestapo took it over for their 'interrogations'. Again in 1989 the neighbourhood was the scene of Berlin's most important protest meetings, held in the 19C red-brick **Gethsemane-Kirche** on Stargarder Strasse.

SCHLOSS CHARLOTTENBURG★★

What began in 1695 as a modest summer residence for the future Queen Sophie Charlotte, fleeing the pomp of the Berliner Schloss, grew with the Hohenzollerns' royal pretensions into the magnificent Baroque palace (BU) that now bears her name. After becoming King Frederick I, her husband instructed architect Johann Friedrich Eosander von Göthe to build the great **dome**, with the goddess of Fortune as its weathervane, and add the **Orangerie** to the west. Baroque master Georg von Knobelsdorff designed the grand **east wing** for the rare occasions when his king, Frederick II, left Potsdam for Berlin.

Andreas Schlüter's **bronze equestrian statue** (1697) of the Great Elector Frederick-William was brought to the palace courtyard in 1952. Originally standing near the Berliner Schloss, it was fished from Lake Tegel, where it had sunk while being moved during the Second World War.

The Schloss has been lovingly restored and appropriately refurbished, using material from other 18C Prussian palaces to replace that which had been destroyed by wartime bombing.

There are one-hour guided tours of the **Royal Apartments** in the central building and west wing. Highlights include the **Porcelain Room★★**, reflecting the 18C taste for Chinese and Japanese porcelain, the **Eichengalerie** (Oak Gallery), in which chamber music recitals are held, the opulent Rococo **Eosanderkapelle★** (Eosander Chapel), and the **Winterkammer★**, apartments used by Frederick-William II and III.

Knobelsdorff's grandiose east wing, **Knobelsdorff Flügel★★**, presently houses the **National Galerie der Romantik★★** (Gallery of Romantic Art) on the ground floor. The

Gladiators guard the main entrance to Schloss Charlottenburg.

great 19C collection, including works by Caspar David Friedrich, Karl Friedrich Schinkel and Carl Blechen, is due to be transferred to the Museumsinsel (*see* p.80) in 1999. Upstairs in the **Golden Gallery★★**, a dazzling ballroom and concert hall, the eight masterly paintings by Watteau, Frederick II's favourite French artist, are staying put.

The **Schlossgarten★★** behind the palace is a charming mixture of formal French gardens and more 'natural' English landscaping. Just beyond the palace's east wing is the 19C **Schinkel Pavilion★**, an Italian-style villa built in 1824 for King Frederick-William III, now a small museum for the art of Schinkel's era. North, beyond the carp pond, is a Baroque **Belvedere★** with a **museum★** which has a display of exquisite pieces from Berlin's royal porcelain factory, Königliche Porzellan-Manufaktur.

With its formal and informal gardens, woodlands, lakes and islands, Schloss Charlottenburg is a popular place of relaxation for Berliners and visitors.

GRUNEWALD★★ AND WANNSEE★★

Stretching south-west from Charlottenburg, the huge pine forest of Grunewald (AUV) was a major source of fuel for the ruined post-war city and, after replanting, became a welcome recreational open space for Walled-in West Berliners in the Cold War years. Chestnut, beech, lime, birch and oak trees have been added to the 18 million pines, and sheltering in the forest's depths is a wealth of protected wildlife – deer, wild boar, foxes and rabbits.

The Lakes★★

There are plenty of opportunities for watersports, the most popular lakes for swimming being **Strandbad Wannsee★★** and **Krumme Lanke**, with their sandy beaches and pleasant lakeshore restaurants, and **Schlachtensee★**, small enough to swim right across. Nails hammered into tree trunks at the water's edge are there for local residents to hang their dressing-gowns on when they come down for their morning dip. In winter,

The lakes around Berlin provide all kinds of water-based recreation.

the lakes usually freeze over hard enough for people to walk or skate across, as in a Brueghel painting.

Jagdschloss Grunewald★
(Grunewald Hunting Lodge)

On the east shore of Grunewaldsee, the 16C lodge was built for Prince-Elector Joachim II, with later Baroque additions, and now houses a collection of Flemish and German paintings, notably by Rubens, Jordaens and **works★★** by Lucas Cranach the Elder.

Pfaueninsel★★ (Peacock Island)

Ferries cross the Havel to this enchanting **park★★** (AV), combining an 18C **arboretum** of ancient oaks and towering lodgepole pines with an **aviary** for golden pheasants, macaws, cockatoos and, yes, peacocks. Landscape architect Peter Josef Lenné laid out the English-style gardens.

Among the island's many fanciful edifices is a fake ruined **castle★**, built by King Frederick-William III's personal carpenter, and a **Schweizer Haus** (Swiss Cottage) by Schinkel, a **Gothic dairy★**, and the **Knights' House** (also by Schinkel).

Haus der Wannsee-Konferenz
(Wannsee Conference Memorial)

A sombre note in this recreation area is struck by the museum installed in the bourgeois villa on the Havel River (*Am Grossen Wannsee 58*) (AV). It was here, on 20 January 1941, that formal plans were drawn up by Hitler's top ministerial officials, under the chairmanship of SS leader Reinhard Heydrich, for the extermination of Europe's Jews. Films, photographs and documents tell the story of the meeting and its aftermath.

SPANDAU★ AND KÖPENICK

These two historic boroughs west and east of the city centre are well worth an exploratory walk, deserving at least a morning or afternoon.

Spandau★

People in this ancient borough on the western edge of town (AU) do not even consider themselves Berliners. Spandau, they are quick to remind you, was here first, citing a documented reference (1197) pre-dating anything the capital can produce by 40 years, with a settlement of Slav peasants recorded from the 8C. Local taxi drivers heading for the city centre talk about 'going to Berlin'. Still very much the country village, the only borough west of the Havel River seems to have more in common with the Brandenburg hinterland than with the metropolis, particularly since reunification.

A stroll through Spandau's Old Town is like stepping back in time.

In the restored **Altstadt**★ (Old Town), the oldest house, with a 15C Gothic vaulted interior, is at Breite Strasse 32, while other fine 17C and 18C houses with gables and arches can be seen in Ritterstrasse and Marktstrasse. The much-restored 15C Gothic **St-Nikolai-Kirche** (St Nicholas' Church) has a Baroque domed lantern on its belfry and a stately Renaissance altar (1581). The 19C bronze statue of Joachim II in front of the church reflects the Spandauers' claim to have pressured the Prince-Elector into adopting the Protestant faith in 1539.

Out in the Havel River, the 16C red-brick **Zitadelle★** (Citadel) was built by Joachim II in grand Renaissance style around the medieval **Juliusturm** (Julius Tower, early 13C) which is Berlin's oldest secular building. The fortress now houses the town's **Stadtgeschichtliches Museum Spandau** (Museum of Local History).

Köpenick

South-east along the Spree, this borough (DV), too, is much older than Berlin, with a Slav settlement dating back to the 9C. It is also the city's largest borough, embracing extensive forests and lakes.

The town's historic centre and castle stand on an island at the confluence of the Spree and its Dahme tributary. Built on the site of a medieval fortress and Joachim II's hunting lodge, ruined in the Thirty Years' War, **Schloss Köpenick** is a fine 17C Baroque castle that now houses part of Berlin's **Kunstgewerbemuseum★★** (Decorative Arts Museum), with Meissen china and royal jewellery displayed among Renaissance and Baroque furniture.

The best of the 18C houses in the **Altstadt** (Old Town) are to be found in Alter Markt square and along Alt-Köpenick street. The **Rathaus** (Town Hall, 1904) is one of Berlin's most impressive brick buildings, with a superb interior courtyard and staircase.

Grosser Müggelsee★★ is the most popular of eastern Berlin's lakes, fine for swimming, fishing, windsurfing and sailing. Perhaps the loveliest of the lakeside walks is **Am langen See★★**, which takes you along the north bank.

MUSEUMS

Since reunification, dozens of Berlin's 150-plus collections are being moved around, renovated and rescued from Cold War storage. The following information reflects the latest decisions of state and city authorities but is inevitably subject to change. The principal museums are to be found in four main areas: Museumsinsel, in eastern Berlin; Charlottenburg, around the Schloss; Tiergarten, in and near the Kulturforum; and Dahlem.

MUSEUMSINSEL★★★ (MUSEUMS ISLAND)

All four museums on the island in the Spree are undergoing extensive renovation.

Altes Museum★★

This museum (PY), designed by Schinkel in 1823, currently stages large-scale special exhibitions. However, it will become the permanent home for the Greek and Roman antiquities collection (Antikensammlung),

The main entrance to the Altes Museum has an imposing Classical columned façade.

Originally devoted to German art, the Alte Nationalgalerie today includes works of 19C and 20C artists from several countries.

previously displayed in Charlottenburg. This important collection includes the famous **Hildesheim★★★** silverware treasure, marble sculptures, and a collection of everyday objects and artefacts from the Greek, Etruscan and Roman civilisations.

Alte Nationalgalerie★★

This museum (PY), according to the façade's nationalist inscription of 1871, is dedicated 'To German Art' (Der Deutschen Kunst), but in fact it includes a range of 19C and 20C art from other countries too, notably the Galerie der Romantik (Gallery of Romantic Art), French and German Impressionists, and early Expressionists.

Bodemuseum★★

At the west end of the island (OY), this domed museum, named after the great art historian and museum director, Wilhelm von Bode (1845-1929), reunites Berlin's sculpture collections spanning Classical antiquity to the Renaissance and Baroque masters.

The Pergamonmuseum, seen from the Spree Canal.

Pergamonmuseum★★★

Am Kupfergraben

This, the star attraction of the Museumsinsel (OY), takes its name from the Pergamum Altar, a Hellenistic masterpiece of the 2C BC transported piece by piece from what is now Bergama, on Turkey's Aegean coast. The immense colonnaded marble **shrine to Zeus★★★** and/or Athena has been reconstructed to fill an entire hall of the museum, together with its sculpted friezes depicting the Greek gods' combats with the Giants. Also installed largely in its original form is the formidable **Babylonian Processional Way** and **Gate of Ishtar★★**, built by King Nebuchadnezzar II (605-562 BC). The goddess Ishtar's lions, carved in relief on the street's ochre- and blue-glazed brick walls, stride towards the gate, bearing the dragons and bulls of the gods, Marduk and Adad.

The third of the museum's great antiquities is the **Gateway to Milet market★★** (c. AD 120). The prosperous port-city in Greek Asia Minor had an appropriately monumental gateway for its shopping mall, combining Ionic and Corinthian columns with Roman arches.

CHARLOTTENBURG

Ägyptisches Museum★★★

(Egyptian Museum)

Schloss-Strasse 70

Berlin's marvellous collection of ancient Egyptian art – sculpture, jewellery and ceramics – spans 3 000 years of Pharaohs and their Greek and Roman successors. The major attraction is the exquisite **bust of Queen Nefertiti★★★** (1340 BC), found at Tell El Amarna in 1914. Renegade Pharaoh Akhenaten's consort was portrayed in what Egyptologists consider a working model – hence the single eye – left in the sculptor's workshop after Tutankhamun moved the royal capital back to Thebes. A more recent acquisition is the grand **Kalabsha Gate★★** (20 BC), rescued in the 1960s from flooding by the Aswan Dam. Roman Emperor Augustus appears in carved relief as a Pharaoh making a sacrifice to the Egyptian gods.

Sammlung Berggruen★★

(Berggruen Collection)

Schloss-Strasse 1

Across the street from the Ägyptisches Museum, this splendid 1996 addition to

Berlin's museum scene bears the subtitle **Picasso und seine Zeit** (Picasso and his Times). On long-term loan from art collector Heinz Berggruen, some 70 paintings and sculptures representative of Picasso's whole career are on show, along with major pieces by six other artists: Van Gogh, Cézanne, Braque, Klee, Henri Laurens and Giacometti.

TIERGARTEN

Gemäldegalerie*** (Gallery of Painting)

Matthäikirchplatz 4

Moved in 1998 to its new building in the Kulturforum (*see* p.63), the museum unites two collections of European paintings (13C-18C) from Dahlem and the Museumsinsel. Highlights include:

Italian: Giotto *Death of Mary* (1310); Botticelli *Mary Enthroned* (1484); Raphael *Mary with Child* and *John the Baptist* (1505); Giorgione *Portrait of a Young Man* (1506); Moroni *The Duke of Albuquerque* (1560); Caravaggio *Amor Vincit Omnia* (1602).

German: Konrad Witz *Queen of Sheba* (1435); Schongauer *Birth of Christ* (1480); Altdorfer *Resting during the Flight into Egypt* (1510); Dürer *Hieronymus Holzschuher* (1526); Cranach *The Fountain of Youth* (1546).

Dutch and Flemish: Van Eyck *Portrait of Giovanni Arnolfini* (1440); Goes *Adoration of the Magi* (1470); Pieter Brueghel *Proverbs* (1559); Rubens *St Sebastian* (1618); Van Dyck *Wealthy Genoese Couple* (1626); Rembrandt *Self Portrait with Velvet Beret* (1634); Vermeer *Glass of Wine* (1660).

French: Georges de La Tour *Peasant Couple* (1620); Poussin *St Matthew* (1640); Watteau *French Comedy and Italian Comedy* (1716).

Spanish: Velázquez *Portrait of Lady* (1633);

Giovanni Battista Moroni's The Duke of Albuquerque (Gemäldegalerie).

Zurbarán *Don Alonso Verdugo* (1635).
English: Joshua Reynolds *George Clive* (1766); Thomas Gainsborough *The Marsham Children* (1787).

Neue Nationalgalerie**

Potsdamer Strasse 50

Housed in a building that Ludwig Mies van der Rohe originally designed as an office building for Cuba, the permanent collection of late-19C and 20C art is on the lower level, while temporary exhibitions are held on the ground floor. Early modern art begins here with Edvard Munch, Picasso and Kokoschka. German painting includes artists of the Brücke (Bridge) movement, Ernst Ludwig Kirchner and Karl Schmidt-Rottluff, Bauhaus artists Paul Klee and Wassily Kandinsky, and Expressionists Max Beckmann, Otto Dix and George Grosz. Major US artists include Morris Louis, Frank Stella and Barnett Newman. On the museum terrace are sculptures by Henry Moore, Alexander Calder and Auguste Renoir.

DAHLEM★★★

Museum für Völkerkunde★★★

(Museum of Ethnography)

Lansstrasse 8, Dahlem

Huge collections of Asian, Indian, African and American pre-Columbian art are housed in the Dahlem museum complex (BV) being vacated by the Gemäldegalerie (*see* p.84). The exhibits, totalling almost 400 000, are arranged in sections according to the origin of the works: **Museum für Islamische Kunst★★**, illustrating Moslem art from the 7C to the 19C; **Abteilung Nord- und Westafrika★★**, with terracotta heads from Ife, Benin bronzes and Berber jewellery; **Museum für Ostasiatische Kunst★**, containing Japanese and Chinese artefacts; **Abteilung Alt-Amerika★★★**, with beautiful artefacts and jewellery from early American civilisations; **Abteilung Südsee★★**, including items from the Pacific and Indonesia; **Abteilung Südasien★**, with south-east Asian, Indian and Sri Lankan theatrical and religious artefacts; **Museum für Deutsche Volkskunde★**, with an assortment of domestic, agricultural and religious pieces; and the **Museum für Indische Kunst★★**, with astonishing religious statuettes.

OTHER ATTRACTIONS

Anhalter Bahnhof (Anhalter Station)
Askanischer Platz
Nostalgic neo-Renaissance façade of the once-celebrated railway station.

Bauhaus-Archiv★, Museum für Gestaltung
Klingerhöferstrasse 14
Walter Gropius' design for the museum of the renowned school for architects, designers, artists and photographers.

Berlin Museum *Lindenstrasse 14*
The city's history, folklore and culture, exhibited in a Baroque courthouse.

The Bauhaus-Archiv is a showcase for Germany's great school of early 20C art and architecture.

Bröhan-Museum★ *Schloss-Strasse 1a*
Jugendstil and art deco furniture, porcelain, glassware, silverware and paintings.

Brücke Museum★ *Bussardsteig 9, Zehlendorf*
Rotating exhibitions taken from a

The Glienicke Bridge, leading to the Volkspark Klein-Glienicke, was used for exchanging eastern and western spies during the Cold War.

permanent collection of the early-20C Dresden art movement: Nolde, Heckel, Schmidt-Rottluff and Kirchner (BV).

Friedrichwerdersche Kirche★
Am Werderschen Markt
Karl Friedrich Schinkel's 1824 English-style Gothic church, restored as the **Schinkel-museum★** recording the architect's life and work.

Institut für Wasserbau und Schiffbau (Hydraulic and Ship Engineering Institute)
Müller-Breslau-Strasse
Ludwig Leo's comically colourful 1976 laboratory building by the Landwehr Canal.

Jüdisches Museum (Jewish Museum)
Lindenstrasse 13
Daniel Libeskind's avant-garde design for the annexe to the Berlin Museum (*see* p.87), documenting the rich contribution of the Jewish community to the city's life.

Volkspark Klein-Glienicke★★
(Klein-Glienicke Estate)
Königstrasse, Wannsee
Enchanting 19C park landscaped by Peter Jospeh Lenné, with a Schloss (castle) by Schinkel.

Lübars *Reinickendorf*
Surrounded by meadows, this is Berlin's own country village, with farmhouses now converted into restaurants.

Ludwigkirchplatz★ *Wilmersdorf*
Pleasant tree-shaded square surrounded by bars, open-air cafés and restaurants.

Märkisches Museum★
Am Köllnischen Park 5, Mitte
A museum devoted to the folklore of Berlin and Brandenburg, with special emphasis on working-class life and the city's rich theatre history.

Museum für Gegenwart-Berlin★★
(Museum of Contemporary Art)
Hamburger Station, Invalidenstrasse 50
Mid-19C railway station restored to house Erich Marx's collection: Beuys, Warhol, Rauschenberg, Haring and Baselitz.

Olympiastadion★ (Olympic Stadium)
Charlottenburg
Hitler's sports stadium (AU), built to seat 120 000 spectators for the 1936 Berlin Olympics. It was spared bombardment to serve as headquarters of the British Army.

Shellhaus *Reichpietschufer 60 (Tiergarten)*
The undulating façade, overlooking the Landwehr Canal, illustrates Emil

Fahrenkamp's innovative design in office building (1930).

Sophienstrasse* *Mitte*
Attractively restored 18C and 19C neo-Renaissance houses, with a view of Sophienkirche's Baroque belfry (PX).

Teddy Museum *Kurfürstendamm 147*
The world's first teddy bear museum, starring Rupert, Winnie the Pooh and Paddington, but also the German aristocrat of cuddlies, the Steiff bear, dating back to 1910.

Tegeler See★★ (Tegel Lake)
Charming lake cruises off the beaten track, with an intriguing view through the trees of the grand Villa Borsig (1911), a pastiche of Potsdam's Sanssouci (*see* p.93).

Wäschereimuseum (Laundry Museum)
Luisenstrasse 23, Köpenick
Since opening the first public laundry in 1835, Köpenick has been Berlin's Waschküche (washing kitchen), documented here with old machinery, irons, wringers and detergents.

EXCURSIONS

POTSDAM

The capital of Brandenburg is in origin, like Spandau and Köpenick, a Slav settlement pre-dating Berlin. Its parks, lakes and palaces make a pleasant excursion, with only the barest reminder that there is a tougher side to Potsdam's past.

In the 18C Frederick-William, the Sergeant King, turned Potsdam into a garrison town where he delighted in watching his beloved Prussian guards goose-stepping on parade. His philosopher son, Frederick II, injected a little culture and refinement by filling his new Schloss Sanssouci (*see* p.93) with musicians, writers and artists. In March 1933 Goebbels highlighted the town's Prussian militarist past by having Field Marshal Hindenburg give Hitler a crypto-religious blessing in the Garnisonkirche (Garrison Church). In 1945, the Allies met in Potsdam to divide up the country. To remove lingering symbols of Prussian militarism, the East German Communists dismantled Hohenzollern

Hitler's Olympic Stadium symbolised Germany's goal of invincible power.

monuments such as the town palace and the Garnisonkirche. In 1991 the church bells were restored – but not the church – and the coffins of the Sergeant King and Frederick II were brought back to be reburied in their favourite town.

The Town★★

Wartime bombing and East German urban planning left little of Potsdam's historic fabric. The most attractive surviving neighbourhood is the 18C red-brick **Holländisches Viertel★** (Dutch Quarter) around Mittelstrasse. Baroque façades are being restored in **Charlottenstrasse★**. Schinkel's imposing 19C **Nikolaikirche★** (St Nicholas's Church) has been rebuilt and Knobelsdorff's graceful **Marstall** (Royal Stables, 1746) has been transformed into a **Cinema Museum★**.

The terraced gardens of Schloss Sanssouci are filled with beautiful sculptures.

Schloss Sanssouci★★★ and Park★★★

Frederick II's own sketches served as a basis for the Rococo design of Georg von Knobelsdorff. An opulent residence with terraced gardens, the 1745 palace was to be a haven of peace where the king could play his music and philosophise away from the cares of state – *sans souci*. Indeed, its most beautiful room is the **Konzertzimmer** (Recital Room) in which Frederick II played his flute, accompanied on the harpsichord by Johann Sebastian Bach's son, Carl Philipp Emmanuel, as depicted in a 19C painting by Adolf von Menzel. The cosy cedarwood **Bibliothek** (Library) containing the king's 2 200 favourite French books is in the east wing rotunda, overlooking the terrace where he planned to be buried – and finally was in 1991. The splendid central **Marmorsaal** (Marble Hall) was where the king held his 'philosophical suppers'. Their star performer, from 1750 to 1753, slept in the west wing in what is now known as the **Voltaire-Zimmer**, redecorated with monkeys and garish birds after the Frenchman fell out of favour.

The charming palace **gardens** and **park**★★★, both formal French and English-landscaped, cover about 300 hectares (nearly 750 acres). East of the palace is the royal **Bildergalerie**★ (Picture Gallery) of works by Italian and Flemish masters, notably Guido Reni, Caravaggio, Van Dyck and Rubens. The **Chinesisches Teehaus**★★ (Chinese Tea House), south-west of the terraced gardens, has gilded palm trees for columns and a gilded mandarin on the roof.

Life-size gilded figures are seated round the palm tree columns surrounding the recently restored Chinese Tea House.

Neues Palais★★

Frederick II commissioned thousands of craftsmen to work on the **Neues Palais★★** (New Palace), intended to show the world that the victorious Prussia had not been damaged by the Seven Years' War (1757-1763). The building, in extravagant and ostentatious Rococo style, provided an ideal setting for the courtiers to strut and parade.

Schloss Cecilienhof★

The ivy-covered, half-timbered house lies north of the city centre in the **Neuer Garten★★** (New Garden), a pleasant 19C park laid out by Peter Josepf Lenné. Built in 1914, more as Victorian country manor than Prussian palace, Cecilienhof hosted the Potsdam Treaty negotiations in July 1945. Now a luxury hotel, it has preserved the conference rooms where Joseph Stalin, Harry Truman and Winston Churchill

The wonderfully extravagant New Palace and its garden have some 428 sculptures.

Schloss Cecilienhof, once home to the Crown Prince and his wife, Cecilia, is now a luxury hotel.

agreed on the division of Germany and the war reparations it would have to pay.

BABELSBERG*

South-west of the city of Berlin, the town is accessed by the S-Bahn Nos 3, 7 Babelsberg. Take bus 691 for Schloss Babelsberg and buses 690 or 692 for the DEFA-Studio Babelsberg.

The original neo-Gothic **Schloss Babelsberg*** (Babelsberg Castle) was designed by Schinkel (1833) as the summer residence of Princess Augusta and the then Prince William. A tour covers the main formal rooms in the castle, culminating in the elegant ballroom. The romantically landscaped **park**** (designed by Lenné) is peppered with medieval and neo-Gothic follies, and the numerous walks through the attractive park afford pleasant views over the Havel and Glienicke Bridge.

To the south of the town is the **DEFA-Studio Babelsberg** (*Grossbeerenstrasse*). Film buffs can find out the secrets behind the special effects of films such as *Jason and the Argonauts* and *Sinbad's Adventures.* The guided tour of the studios includes staged stunts but admission is expensive.

WEATHER

In Germany, Berlin has always been renowned for the quality of its air. It has a tonic freshness that prompts people to sleep, summer and winter, with the window open. Heavy traffic days can, as in any metropolis these days, create pollution in the city centre or on the Autobahn. The climate is continental, i.e. crisp and cold in winter, cold enough to freeze over the lakes in January, but healthily dry. Summers are warm, surprisingly hot, but not oppressively humid. Spring and autumn have their rains, brought by the prevailing westerly winds, but nothing drearily prolonged (averaging 500-600mm per year.

CALENDAR OF EVENTS

January

Internationale Grüne Woche (International Green Week) Gardening and agricultural fair, offering specialities of German and international cuisine.

February

International Filmfestspiele Berlin's International Film Festival is one of the big three, with Cannes and Venice.

March

Internationale Tourismus-Börse (ITB) The world's biggest international tourism fair.

Musik-Biennale Biennial music festival at the Staatsoper.

April

Berliner Kunsttage (fine arts festival) Street-art and open house in the galleries.

Easter Week.

Opera Festival at the Staatsoper.

May

Theatertreffen (Theatre Rendezvous) Two

weeks of top German-language drama.

June

Parkfestspiele Potsdam Arts festival in Sanssouci gardens.

Treptow in Flammen (Treptow in Flames) Fireworks festival.

July

Love Parade, boisterous Kurfürstendamm and Tiergarten music parade: techno, hip-hop and more.

Bach Tage (Bach Festival).

August

Kreuzberger Festliche Tage Kreuzberg street festival.

September

Funkausstellung (electronics fair) Held every odd-number year.

Berliner Festwochen Berlin theatre and arts festival.

Berlin Marathon.

October

JazzFest International jazz festival in Haus der Kulturen der Welt.

November

Antiquitätenmesse (Antiques Fair).

Spirits run high at the St Christopher's day street parade.

ACCOMMODATION

As in other major European cities, there is no shortage of accommodation in Berlin but hotels tend to be rather expensive in comparison, with only a few more modestly priced boarding-house-style *Hotel-Garni* or *Pension.* A choice of options can be found all over the city but there is a concentration of hotels around the Ku'damm and Charlottenburg. Many large, expensive hotels can be found in the Mitte district. Lower-price accommodation tends to be

centred in Schöneberg and Kreuzberg. Prices per double room per night are as follows:
5 star: up to 600DM
4 star: up to 400DM
3 star: up to 300DM
2 star: up to 200DM
1 star: under 150DM
Breakfast is usually, but not always, included in the price.

Contact Berlin Tourismus Marketing GmbH for hotel reservations and information ☎ **(030) 25 00 25**.

Reservations for any hotel, inn or boarding-house in Germany can be made through the central German booking office: Allgemeine Deutsche Zimmerreservierung (ADZ), Corneliusstraße 34, D-60325 Frankfurt am Main ☎ **(069) 74 07 67**.

There are a number of **youth hostels** in Berlin. For information, contact Deutsches Jugendherbergswerk Hauptverband, Bismarckstraße 8, D-32756 Detmold ☎ **(052 31) 741 10**. An International Youth Hostel Federation card will be required for most hostels.

Recommendations

500–600DM

At the top of the range are the newly re-opened **Hotel Adlon**, Unter den Linden 77 (☎ **2 26 10**), with a splendid view of the Brandenburg Gate; its sister hotel, the **Kempinski Hotel Bristol**, Kurfürstendamm 27 (☎ **88 43 40**), centrally located for the city's best shopping and entertainment; and the ultra-modern **Grand Hotel Esplanade**, Lützowufer 15 (☎ **25 47 80**), overlooking the Landwehr Canal. In the Grunewald area is the **Schlosshotel Vier Jahreszeiten**,

Brahmsstrasse 10 (☎ **89 58 40**), a reconstructed palace dating from the period of the Emperor William II, with period furniture.

300–400DM
Charmingly situated in Kreuzberg is **Riehmers Hofgarten**, Yorckstrasse 83 (☎ **78 10 11**). The **Brandenburger Hof**, Eislebenerstrasse 14 (☎ **21 40 50**) is a modernised city palace, with a delightful inner courtryard garden and furnished in Bauhaus style.

Moderately expensive is **Askanischer Hof**, Kurfürstendamm 53 (☎ **8 81 80 33**), a fine old-fashioned *Hotel-Garni* with Jugendstil (art nouveau) décor. The **Bleibtreu-Hotel**, Bleibtreustrasse 31 (☎ **88 47 40**) is a modernised city house furnished in the Designer style, with a pleasant inner courtyard garden area.

Situated in a beautiful location on the bend in the river Spree known as the Spreebogen is the **Sorat Hotel Spreebogen**, Alt Moabit 99 (☎ **39 92 00**), a modern hotel in a converted dairy.

200–300DM
Germany's largest hotel, the **Estrel Residence**, Sonnenallee 225 (☎ **6 83 10**), has an interesting design, with some 1125 rooms, 80 suites and three restaurants (including Italian and Thai).

In contrast is the small **Hotel Villa Toscana**, Bahnhofstrasse 19, Lichterfelde (☎ **7 68 92 70**), an intimate villa furnished

Hotel Adlon, the top-of-the-range palace-hotel frequented by many famous personalities such as Charlie Chaplin.

in Italian style and set in a beautiful garden.

In the middle of Grunewald forest, sample the rustic comfort of **Forsthaus Paulsborn**, Hüttenweg 90, (☎ **8 18 19 10**).

FOOD AND DRINK

The renewal of its status as the national capital – once again a cosmopolitan city – and the influx of more and more foreign visitors have resulted in Berlin becoming increasingly ambitious about its cuisine. The city's Italian, French, Turkish and Asian restaurants are of the highest quality and German traditional dishes are being prepared with more delicacy, while portions remain as generous as ever.

Soups Berlin's favourite soup is *Linsensuppe*, which includes lentils with slices of sausage. *Bohnensuppe* (bean soup) combines several

The Nikolai Quarter offers out-of-door dining overlooking the Spree.

different kinds of beans, while the best *Kartoffelsuppe* is more than just potato soup, including celery, leeks and parsnips. *Leberknödelsuppe* is made with ox-liver dumplings, with onions and garlic.

Main Dishes The Havel River provides freshwater fish, in particular a pike-perch (*Havelzander*) usually served with boiled potatoes (*Salzkartoffel*), and eel cooked in a dill sauce (*Havelaal grün*). Potatoes are a Berlin speciality, never more delicious than as potato pancakes (*Kartoffelpuffer*), crisply fried and served with slightly tart apple sauce (*Apfelmus*).

Three Berlin meat dishes stand out: smoked pork chops known as *Kasseler Rippen*, originating not in the city of Kassel but named after Herr Kassel, a Berlin butcher; *Eisbein mit Sauerkraut*, pig's knuckle with Sauerkraut cooked in white wine with juniper berries and cloves; and the solid working-man's dish of *gebratene Leber*, ox liver sizzling with onion rings and slices of apple.

Snacks Midnight, midday – any time is good for a Berlin stand-up meal of *Buletten*, tangy meatballs considered vastly superior to the hamburger; *Currywurst*, sausage dipped in a curry sauce; or the increasingly popular Turkish Döner, spit-roasted sliced mutton in pitta-bread.

Dessert Dresden plum cake (*Pflaumenkuchen*) is always a favourite, but try a *compote* of red fruits – raspberries, blackcurrants and cherries – known as *Rote Grütze*, served with cream or vanilla sauce.

Drinks Berliners like their local beers –

Schultheiss or Warburger – on tap (*vom Fass*) or bottled as Pils, light and strong, Export, light and smooth, or Bock, dark and thick. In summer Berliner Weisse is a draught beer served pink with a shot of raspberry syrup or liqueur, or green with woodruff syrup (*Waldmeister*). In winter they 'chase' their beer with a shot of schnapps – clear potato, corn or barley alcohol.

Recommendations

Complete listings are to be found in the *Michelin Red Guide Deutschland* but here are a few suggestions by neighbourhood:

Kurfürstendamm and Savignyplatz

Bovril (Kurfürstendamm 184 ☎ **881 8461**) Elegant French bistro.
Florian (Grolmannstrasse 52 ☎ **313 9184**) Popular with writers and actors; refined South German cuisine.
Shell (Knesebeckstrasse 22 ☎ **312 8310**) Excellent Italian cuisine; cheerful service with fashionable clientele.
Spree-Athen (Leibnitzstrasse 60 ☎ **3 24 17 33**) Restaurant in the Old Berlin style with entertainment featuring, among other things, popular chansons and music from the Imperial era.

Wilmersdorf

Wirtshaus Nussbaum (Bundesplatz 5 ☎ **8 54 50 20**) Berlin bar modelled on the original popular haunt Zilles.

Kreuzberg

Riehmers (Hagelberger Strasse 9 ☎ **786 8608**) Good German cuisine in the pretty setting of the Riehmers Hofgarten.
Exil (Paul-Lincke Ufer 44 ☎ **612 7037**)

Austrian cuisine, lively and relaxed, with views of the Landwehr Canal.
Monte Croce (Mittenwalderstrasse 6 ☎ **694 3968**) First-class Italian peasant fare, chef's choice-of-the-day, served in traditional Berlin *Hinterhof* (rear courtyard).

Mitte
Opernpalais (Unter den Linden 5 ☎ **20 26 84 43**) Residence of the daughter of Queen Luise, completely and historically accurately renovated.
Borchardt (Französische Strasse 47 ☎ **20 39 71 17**) Former wine tavern with generously-sized four-pillared restaurant area, serving late after-theatre dinner.
Reinhard's (Poststrasse 28 ☎ **242 5295**) Art deco atmosphere of the golden 20s, with a refined cosmopolitan cuisine.
Oren (Oranienburger Strasse 28 ☎ **282 8228**) Bustling restaurant serving Jewish meals next to the synagogue.

Zehlendorf
Blockhaus Nikolskoe (Nikolskoer Weg ☎ **805 2914**) Fine food in lakeside timbered Russian *datcha.*

Steglitz
Maxwell (Bergstrasse 22 ☎ **2 80 71 21**) Former brewery within a farmstead in turn-of-the-century style.

Wannsee
Remise (Königstrasse 36 ☎ **8 05 40 00**) Outhouse at Glienicke Castle, with a magnificent park garden area.

Cafés
Hegel (Savignyplatz 2) Old-world

atmosphere (and bortsch-soup) attracting Russian émigrés and their groupies.
Savigny (Grolmannstrasse 53) Fashionable hang-out overlooking Landwehr Canal.
Einstein (Kurfürstenstrasse 58) Elegant Viennese coffee house with garden, 1900s atmosphere, international newspapers and excellent coffee.
Kranzler (Kurfürstendamm/Joachimsthalerstrasse) Institution now popular with tourists and elderly ladies hooked on pastries.
Ici (Auguststrasse 61) Lively attractive meeting place for artists in heart of old eastern Berlin.
Obs & Gemüse (Oranienburger Strasse 48) Former grocery shop popular with eastern Berlin's younger crowd.

SHOPPING

For over 50 years, since the Second World War, Berlin (or at least half of it) has been a shop window for the consumer world of the west. European and American visitors have always found that the best of their own goods have been available in the boutiques and department stores around the Kurfürstendamm, Tauentzienstrasse and Wittenbergplatz. So what is there specifically German to buy here to take home?

Toys

For all the jazzy attractions of electronic games, good old **electric trains** still have enormous appeal, and the German versions are quite simply the best in the world. The national technological skills also go into model spaceships, aircraft and boats. There are **construction kits** for children – or their parents – to build their own Schloss Charlottenburg or Sanssouci. Even modern architects have got in on the act, with sets of multi-coloured Bauhaus building blocks with which to create your own Mies van der Rohe skyscraper. **Dolls** come dressed in traditional costume from every region in Germany, and the **teddy bears** and other cuddly animals are particularly appealing.

Porcelain

One of the up-market benefits of reunification has been the availability once more of original designs for eastern Germany's **Meissen** china, sold in its own boutique at Kurfürstendamm 214. The elegant modern designs of **Rosenthal** china are at No 226, and Berlin's own royal porcelain factory, **Königliche Porzellan Manufaktur** (KPM), sells its wares at No 26a – though it is now officially known as the Staatliche Porzellan Manufaktur. For the child that you are dying to spoil, there are even exorbitantly-priced miniature china sets for dolls' houses.

The 13m (40ft) high 'water-clock' in the Europa-Center.

Antiques

Some good 19C **Biedermeyer** and early-20C **Jugendstil** or 1920s **Art Deco** furniture and glassware are coming out of eastern German attics but the dealers know their value and there are no amazing bargains to be had. If you just enjoy browsing, look around the shops near the Schloss Charlottenburg, Bleibtreu, Schlüter and Mommsenstrasse, or in Eisenach Strasse in Schöneberg.

Flea Markets

Seek out bargains among the junk and kitsch at one of the street markets:
Grosser Berliner Trödel- und Kunstmarkt (Strasse des 17 Juni, Charlottenburg) Open Saturday and Sunday 8am-4pm.
Antik- & Flohmarkt Mitte (under the elevated railway arches of Bahnhof Friedrichstrasse) Open daily 11am-6pm, except Tuesday.
Berliner Kunst- und Nostalgie markt (beneath the awnings along Kupfergraben, on the Museumsinsel).
Flohmarkt Am Fehrbelliner Platz (Fehrbelliner Platz, Wilmersdorf) Open Saturday and Sunday 8am-4pm.
Kunst & Trödelmarkt (Schönhauser Allee 36/38).
Pariser Platz Market (Pariser Platz, Mitte) Open daily, 9am-dusk.

ENTERTAINMENT AND NIGHTLIFE

Competing with Berliners for concert and theatre tickets is not easy, so try to book in advance for major events through a travel agency before leaving home. Tickets can be booked from home by calling Berlin Tourismus Marketing ☎ **(030) 25 00 25** Fax **(030) 25 00 24 24**, or in Berlin at **Theaterkasse**, Hardenbergstrasse 6, Charlottenburg ☎ **312 70 41** Fax **312 70 83/312 65 53**. Besides the tourist office's *Berlin Programm*, three excellent 'What's On' city-magazines, *Tip*, *Prinz* and *Zitty*, provide full listings of music and theatre events.

To hear the great **Berlin Philharmonic Orchestra** in the matchless acoustic and visual setting of the Philharmonie concert hall in the Kulturforum is an unforgettable experience. **Chamber music** is equally well served in the **Kammermusiksaal** at the rear of the Philharmonie but also in the **Akademie der Künste** in the Hansaviertel and the **Hochschule der Künste** at Hardenbergstrasse 33.

Opera has three locations in the city: the **Deutsche Staatsoper** at Unter den Linden 5, the **Deutsche Oper** at Bismarckstrasse 35 and the **Komische Oper** at Behrenstrasse 55-57.

The Deutsche Staatsoper is one of Berlin's three venues for opera.

Techno, **rock** and all the variations of world music can be heard in the open air at the Waldbühne, in Charlottenburg, or indoors at the Deutschland-halle at Messedamm 26, or in the Franz-Club at Schönhauser Allee 36-39. Berlin never sleeps and there is an ever-changing **disco** and **nightclub** scene. The city is known as the techno capital and, if this remixed synthetic music is your thing, head for the Mitte and Prenzlauer areas, east of the Brandenburg Gate. Give it a try at **E-Werk** (Wilhelmstrasse 43), **+B+** (Albrechtstrasse 24), or **Tresor/ Globus** (Leipziger Strasse 126a), all in Mitte.

If your command of German is up to it, try the **satirical cabaret** at **Bar Jeder Vernunft** (Schaperstrasse 24) which has good satirical comedy and songs, both modern and from the 1920s; **Distel** (Friedrichstrasse 101), perhaps the only important satirical cabaret to have survived in eastern Berlin before *and* after the fall of the Wall; **Stachelschweine** (Europa-Center) which has a resident group of traditional broad political satire; and **Wühlmäuse**

Cabaret – a Berlin Phenomenon

Berlin, always bitter-sweet, tough and irreverent, is cabaret's natural home. In the great heyday of the 1920s many of the era's leading artists, writers and musicians were involved in its most creative productions.

When director Max Reinhardt opened the cabaret **Schall und Rauch** (Noise and Smoke) on the ground-floor of his new theatre, the Grosses Schauspielhaus in 1919, avant-garde artists **George Grosz** and **John Heartfield** designed the programme for the première. Satirist **Kurt**

Tucholsky, and poets **Walter Mehring** and **Klabund** wrote seering political sketches and songs, complemented by the gentler humour of writer-composer **Friedrich Hollaender**.

Cabaret performers like **Paul Graetz**, classical street-wise Berliner, **Gussy Holl**, stunning blond and witty *femme fatale*, and the breezy, down-to-earth **Claire Waldoff** were the biggest stars in town. Operetta singer **Trude Hesterberg** converted to the more creative work of her own cabaret, **Wilde Bühne** (Savage Stage) at the Theater des Westens, using as one of her writers the still-unknown **Bert Brecht**.

The German Communist Party sponsored cabaret as agitprop to further the Marxist cause, notably **Kabarett der Komiker**, where **Erich Kästner** and **Erich Weinert** wrote militant songs and sketches.

Over on the Kurfürstendamm, five years before she was to become the epitome of Berlin cabaret performers in her film, *The Blue Angel*, **Marlene Dietrich** was trying out as a singer and dancer for the **Nelson Revue**. While other cabarets concentrated on political and social satire – against war-mongers, black-marketeers, ruthless capitalists – the Nelson brothers preferred lighter, more sexy songs, but still with a sting in the tail. Typical was the unladylike longing of saucy **Käthe Erlholz** for an all-conquering Mongol brute like Tamerlaine rather than her usual bald-headed, pot-bellied currency speculators.

Today, Berlin's torch of political and social satire is carried in such cabarets as **Stachelschweine** (Porcupines), **Wühlmäuse** (Voles) and most innovatively at **Bar Jeder Vernunft** (Beyond All Reason). And the songs of Tucholsky, Hollaender and Klabund have been revived with a modern touch by film and theatre actresses **Meret Becker** and **Eleonore Weisgerber**. With Bonn moving its government to Berlin, there is certain to be plenty of new material for the satirists.

Left: Marlene Dietrich plays the role of cabaret singer Lola-Lola in 'The Blue Angel' (1930), a film which launched her career in America.

(Nürnberger Strasse 33) which has satire with guest-artists.

The best **theatre** is to be seen at the Schaubühne at Kurfürstendamm 153, Brecht's Berliner Ensemble at Schiffbauerdamm, Deutsches Theater on Schumannstrasse 13a, and the Volksbühne at Rosa-Luxemburg-Platz. Theater des Westens stages musical comedies.

SPORTS

There are plenty of opportunities for swimming, sailing, windsurfing and other **watersports** on the city's lakes – Wannsee, Schlachtensee, Halensee and Müggelsee. You can **swim** along the Havel, though it is advisable to swim at the supervised beaches: Lieper Bucht, just west of Havelchaussee, and further south at Grosse Steinlanke. If you prefer to swim in a pool, there are swimming pools at Blub (Buschkrugallee 64), a large water park with a 120m slide; the municipal baths at Stadtbad Charlottenburg (Krumme Strasse 6a-8); or summer outdoor bathing at Sommerbad Kreuzberg (Gitschiner Strasse 18-31) or the Olympic Stadium swimming pool.

Boat trips are a great way to get a different view of the city and its surrounding country. For the historical centre and around the Tiergarten take a cruise on a circuit of the Spree and Landwehrkanal. Start out either from the Schlossbrücke (Castle Bridge) in Charlottenburg, or Kupfergraben at the Museumsinsel in the old city centre. Other boats cruise Wannsee, the Müggelsee, Tegeler See and the Unterhavel (Lower Havel) between Spandau and Potsdam. From spring 1998 a new Spree river-bus service will run every 30 minutes between

Nikolaiviertel and Tegler See, via the Tiergarten and Schloss Charlottenburg, with a shuttle connection to Berlin's Tegel airport – 72 minutes all the way, but much cheaper than a cruise or a taxi.

Bicycling is a good way of getting around town – and getting some exercise. You will find that the city has a good network of cycle tracks (indicated by a red stripe on the pavement). Bikes can be rented at the Europa-Center or at several other bike-hire companies. Ask at the tourist office.

There are **ice-skating** rinks in Wilmersdorf and Charlottenburg but opening hours vary so check before you go. For **tennis** there are two city clubs, Rot-Weiss in the Grunewald (Gottfried-von-Cramm-Weg 47), and Blau-Weiss in Wilmersdorf (Waldmeisterstrasse 10-20); ask your hotel or the tourist office about facilities for temporary membership. **Golf** is available at Wannsee Club but it is hard to beat a **hike** in the Grunewald or Tegel Forest, or a **jog** in the Tiergarten, which provide exercise in a scenic setting.

The Olympic Stadium swimming pool is a popular spot for cooling off in summer.

THE BASICS

Before You Go

A valid passport or a personal identity card (for residents of the EU) is sufficient for entry into Germany. Nationals from Australia, Canada, New Zealand and the US may travel within Germany for up to three months without a visa providing they hold a valid passport. No vaccinations are necessary.

Getting There

By Air: There are regular international flights in and out of Berlin's three airports: Tegel airport (TXL) ☎ **(030) 410 11**, Infoline ☎ **(030) 41 01 23 06**; Schönefeld airport (SXF) ☎ **(030) 609 10**, Infoline ☎ **(030) 60 91 12/66**; Tempelhof airport (THF) ☎ **(030) 695 10**, Infoline ☎ **(030) 62 51 22 88**. Most scheduled and charter flights arrive at Tegel; Tempelhof mainly handles charter and domestic flights; Schönefeld mainly handles flights to and from Russia and Eastern Europe.

Lufthansa (☎ **(03) 45 73 77 47** from anywhere in the world), Germany's international airline, offers the most frequent and versatile service, linking Germany with over 160 countries worldwide. Their Berlin office is at Kurfürstendamm 220, 10719 Berlin ☎ **(030) 88 75 88**.

By Car: Travellers from abroad with a national or international licence and a national or international permit may use their car for up to a year in Germany. By road from the UK, Germany can be reached via France, Belgium, Holland or Luxembourg. All motorways lead on to the Berliner Ring and there are well-signposted exits to all parts of the city.

By Coach: Coach connections are available between Berlin and most German cities and several major cities in Europe. Eurolines international coach services run regular bus services to Berlin from Britain and other European countries. Information and bookings in the UK from 52 Grosvenor Gardens, London SW1W 0AU ☎ **(0171) 730 8235**.
The terminus for long-distance coaches is the Central Bus Station in Charlottenburg, Messedamm 8 ☎ **(030) 301 80 28** for information.

By Train: International rail connections link Berlin with several major European cities. At present, Berlin's only international rail terminus is Zoo Station in Charlottenburg. The *Deutsche Bahn* (DB) is Germany's major passenger network and information can be obtained from any of their ticket offices, in DB-licensed travel bureaux or by ringing German Rail Telesales ☎ **(0181) 390 8833** in the UK or ☎ **(030) 194 19** from Berlin. High-speed connections between London Waterloo and Aachen and Cologne can be made via Eurostar.

The Kaiser Wilhelm Memorial Church, seen through the symbolic sculpture simply called 'Berlin'.

A-Z

Arriving
From Tegel airport, buses run every five or ten minutes to Zoo Station and Ku'damm, taking about 35 minutes. Taxis will take half the time and cost around 30DM.

There is a tourist information office in the main hall, open 5.15am-10pm daily.

Accidents and Breakdowns
The Automobile Club ADAC provides assistance in the major cities of Germany, including Berlin. For information, ☎ **01 805 10 11 12**; for breakdown service, ☎ **(01 802) 22 22 22**.

In the event of a breakdown on a motorway, a patrol can be summoned from one of the emergency telephone posts. When telephoning, ask for 'Strassenwachthilfe'. In an emergency, ☎ **110**.

When travelling in a hire car, contact the rental firm in the event of an accident or breakdown.
See also **Driving**

Accommodation see **p.97**

Airports
see **Getting There p.112**

Banks
Banks are usually open on weekdays 8.30am-12.30/1pm and 2.30pm-4pm (5.30/6pm on Thursday); they also open two evenings during the week – days variable from bank to bank. Generally they are closed on Saturday and Sunday although some remain open late at night and during the weekend. Bureaux de change offer better rates of exchange than banks.

Bicycles
Cycling is very popular in Berlin which has about 800km of cycle tracks, marked as a red stripe on the pavement. It is advisable not to walk along these tracks or to stop on them as cyclists travel along them at speed. Consult the guide *ADFC Fahrradstadtplan* or the Yellow Pages (Gelbe Seiten) to find

bicycle-hire outlets.

Bicycles may be taken on the S-Bahn at any time and at certain times on the U-Bahn (*see* **Transport**).

Books

Here are a few suggestions for your holiday reading:

Berlin Alexanderplatz, Alfred Döblin
Goodbye to Berlin, Christopher Isherwood
Mr Norris Changes Train, Christopher Isherwood
The Blue Angel, Heinrich Mann
The Gift, Vladimir Nabokov
Berlin Diary, William L Schirer
The Spy Who Came in from the Cold, John le Carré

Breakdowns *see* Accidents

Buses *see* Transport

Camping

Full details of campsites in Germany can be obtained from the Deutscher Camping Club (DCC), Mandlestrasse 28, D-80802 Munich, or from Camping and Zeitplätze ☎ **(030) 218 60 71**. There are four or five DCC campsites around Berlin.

Car Hire

International car hire companies are based in the city centre as well as at Tegel airport. Make sure that collision damage waiver is included in the insurance. Automatics should be reserved in advance and are more expensive.

The lower age limit for hiring a car is 21 but few international companies hire to drivers under 23, or even 25. Drivers must have held their full licence for at least a year.

With the exception of Avis, there is an upper age limit of 60-65. Unless paying by credit card, a substantial cash deposit is usually required.

See also **Accidents and Breakdowns, Driving** and **Tourist Information Offices**

Children

Places likely to appeal to children in particular include:

The Dahlem Museums (Arnimallee 23-7) Here there is a section aimed at older children, and the Ethnology Museum has a number of exciting exhibits such as masks, puppets and boats.

Berlin Zoo and Aquarium (Budapester Strasse) Two separate establishments next to each other, including a playground.

Blub (Berlin Luft und Badeparadies) (Buschkrugallee 64) A wave-pool, waterfalls, slides and other kinds of water fun.

Deutsches Technik Museum (Transport and Technology Museum) (Kreuzberg, Trebbiner Strasse) Cars, boats and planes of all kinds, with lots of hands-on experiences.
Tierpark Berlin-Friedrichfelde (Am Tierpark 125) Another, very extensive, zoo in the eastern suburb of Friedrichfelde.
Ufa-Fabrik (Viktoriastrasse 10-13, Tempelhof) A farm and multimedia cultural centre.

Churches see **Religion**

Climate see **p. 96**

Clothing

In general Germans dress casually (yet often smartly and stylishly) and there is seldom any need for formal wear. A jacket and tie is required in casinos, however, and in many discos jeans and trainers are prohibited.

Women's sizes

UK	8	10	12	14	16	18
Europe	36	38	40	42	44	46
US	6	8	10	12	14	16

Men's suits

UK/US	36	38	40	42	44	46
Europe	46	48	50	52	54	56

Men's shirts

UK/US	14	14.5	15	15.5	16	16.5	17
Europe	36	37	38	39/40	41	42	43

Men's shoes

UK	7	7.5	8.5	9.5	10.5	11
Europe	41	42	43	44	45	46
US	8	8.5	9.5	10.5	11.5	12

Women's shoes

UK	4.5	5	5.5	6	6.5	7
Europe	38	38	39	39	40	41
US	6	6.5	7	7.5	8	8.5

A horse-drawn tourist bus serves the medieval Nikolaiviertel district.

Consulates *see* Embassies

Consulates see Embassies

Crime

Violent crime is rare in Berlin but, as in any city, sensible precautions should be taken.

- Carry as little money, and as few credit cards, as possible, and leave any valuables in the hotel safe.
- Carry wallets and purses in secure pockets inside your outer clothing, wear body belts, and carry handbags across your body or firmly under your arm.
- Cars, particularly hire cars, can be a target for opportunists, so never leave your car unlocked, and hide away or, better still, remove items of value.
- If your passport is lost or stolen, report it to your Consulate or Embassy at once.

Customs and Entry Regulations

There is no limit on the importation into Germany of tax-paid goods bought in an EU country, provided they are for personal consumption, with the exception of alcohol and tobacco which have fixed limits governing them.

Disabled Visitors

In general adequate facilities for disabled visitors are available in public places, although those in the western part of the city tend to be better than those in the east.

Useful addresses include: Landesamt für Zentrale Soziale Aufgaben, Sächsische Straße 28-30, ☎ **(030) 867 61 14**. Service-Ring-Berlin e.V. ☎ **(030) 322 40 20**.

The *Michelin Red Guide Deutschland* indicates which hotels have facilities for the disabled.

In Britain, RADAR, at 12 City Forum, 250 City Road, London EC1V 8AF; ☎ **(0171) 250 3222**, publishes fact sheets, as well as an annual guide to facilities and accommodation overseas, including Germany.

The German National Tourist office in your own country is a good source of advance information, and you are also advised to check with hotels and travel companies to see that your individual needs can be met.

Driving

A car is not the best way of getting around a busy city and Berlin is no exception.

Drivers should carry a full national (or preferably international) driving licence, insurance documents including a green card (no longer compulsory for EU members but strongly recommended), registration papers for the car, and a nationality sticker for the car rear.

You are required by law to carry a warning triangle with you and it is advisable to adjust the headlight beam to dip to the right.

The minimum age for driving is 18, and cars drive on the right.

Away from main roads, cars give way to those approaching from the right.

The wearing of seat belts both in the front and rear is compulsory.

Children up to 4 years of age must have a special seat; those up to 12 years of age or under 1.5m in height must have a booster cushion. Children under 12 are not allowed to travel in the front seats.

The blood alcohol limit is 0.8%.

There are no tolls on motorways.

Speed limits are as follows:

- Maximum in built-up areas: 50kph/31mph (sometimes 30kph/19mph)
- Maximum outside built-up areas: 100kph/62mph
- The recommended maximum motorway speed is 130kph/81mph
- Cars pulling trailers (including caravans) are limited to a maximum of 80kmh/50mph on roads and motorways

Electric Current

The voltage in Germany is 220V. Sockets are of the two-pin variety and American appliances will require a transformer.

Embassies

American Embassy
Neustädtische Kirchstrasse 4/5, 10117 Berlin
☎ **(030) 238 51 74**

Australian Embassy
Kempinski Plaza, Uhlandstrasse 181/3, 10623 Berlin
☎ **(030) 880 08 80**

British Embassy
Unter den Linden 32/4, 10117 Berlin ☎ **(030) 20 18 40**

Canadian Embassy
Friedrichstrasse 95, 10117 Berlin,
☎ **(030) 261 11 61**

Emergencies

Police ☎ **110**
Fire brigade ☎ **112**
Medical emergencies ☎ **1 00 31**
Dental emergency and all-night chemist ☎ **0 11 41**

Etiquette

There are few differences in culture that visitors need be

aware of but it is polite to remember the following conventions:

- On entering and leaving a shop say *Guten Tag* (good day) and *Auf Wiedersehen* (goodbye).
- Use the 'Sie' form of address if you speak German.
- Shake hands when you greet someone.
- Do not jump the lights at pedestrian crossings or jaywalk (this in fact can incur an on-the-spot fine if you are caught).

Guidebooks see **Maps**

Health
UK nationals should carry a Form E111 which is produced by the Department of Health and entitles the holder to free urgent treatment for accident or illness in EU countries (forms are available from post offices in the UK). In exchange for this form, the German Health Insurance Service (AOK) will give you a form entitling you to free health care. As this does not cover all medical expenses, all foreign nationals, including those from the UK, are advised to take out comprehensive insurance cover, and to keep all bills, receipts and invoices to support any claim.

Hours see **Opening Hours**

Information see **Tourist Information Offices**

A cruise boat explores the shady waters of the Landwehrkanal.

Yes / Ja	White wine / Der Weisswein
No / Nein	Red wine / Der Rotwein
Please / Bitte	Beer / Das Bier
Thank you / Danke	How much does it cost? / Wieviel kostet es?
Good morning / Guten Morgen	Bill / Die Rechnung
Good evening / Guten Abend	Do you speak English? / Sprechen Sie Englisch?
Goodbye / Auf Wiedersehen	Where is … ? / Wo ist … ?
Large / Gross	I don't understand / Ich verstehe nicht
Small / Klein	
Menu / Die Speisekarte	
Water / Das Wasser	

Language
English is becoming increasingly widely spoken in Berlin (rather less so in the eastern part of the city) but an attempt at a few basic phrases in German will always be appreciated.

Lost Property
Central lost property office: Fundbüro der Polizei, Platz der Luftbrücke 6, ☎ **(030) 69 90**
BVG lost property office: Lorenzweg 5, ☎ **(030) 751 80 21**
Deutsche Bahn ☎ **(030) 29 72 96 12**

Maps and Guidebooks
The *Michelin Red Guide Deutschland* contains detailed information on hotels and restaurants throughout Germany, including Berlin, with town plans. The *Michelin Green Guide Berlin* has background information on the city, detailed street maps, descriptions of the attractions and sights within the city and the surrounding area. The Road Map **416** will help you plan your route if driving to Berlin or making excursions from the city.

Medical Care *see* **Health**

Money
The German unit of currency is the Deutsche Mark (DM), divided into 100 Pfennig. Bank notes come in denominations of 5, 10, 20, 50, 100, 200, 500 and 1 000 DM; coins in 1, 2

and 5 DM, and 1, 2 5, 10 and 50 Pfennig. There is no limit to the amount of Deutsche Mark or any other foreign currency that may be taken into or out of Germany.

ECU cards and international credit cards provide immediate access to cash from cash machines 24 hours a day. Payment can be made almost everywhere by EU card, Eurocheque or any of the major credit card companies. Travellers' cheques in US Dollars and major European currencies are accepted, although DM travellers' cheques are preferred.

Throughout Germany, 15 per cent VAT is levied on goods and services; prices quoted include this tax.
See also **Banks**

Newspapers

A wide selection of foreign-language newspapers and magazines can be bought at Internationale Presse Kiosk, Hardenbergstrasse, open 8am-midnight, and around Zoo Station. Most large hotels and news-stands also stock the major European dailies and the *International Herald Tribune,* published in Paris, which offers the latest stock market news from America as well as world news.

The English-language weekly, *Metropolis,* lists everything that goes on in Berlin. Events are also publicised in *BerlinBerlin,* a German/English magazine; both are available from tourist information offices and magazine stands.

Opening Hours

Shops are open 9am-8pm Monday to Friday and 9am-4pm on Saturday. Most of the Turkish shops in Kreuzberg and Neukölln are open later on Saturdays and on Sundays 1pm-5pm.

Chemists Pharmacies (*Apotheke*) are open during

The charming Nikolaiviertel.

normal business hours. Branches with late opening times are posted in the window (*see also* **Emergencies**).

Museums and galleries
Opening times of these vary, but generally they open 9am/10am-5pm daily. Often, they will be closed on Mondays.
See also **Banks** and **Post Offices**

Photography

Good-quality film and camera equipment are available in Berlin and facilities for fast processing are plentiful.

Before taking photographs in museums and art galleries it is wise to check with staff, as photography may be restricted in these places, particularly State museums.

Police

Police (*Polizei*) stations can be found in each district of the city. The main office is at Fundbüro der Polizei, Platz de Luftbrücke 6.

Post Offices

Opening hours are 8am-6pm Monday to Friday; Saturday 8am-noon. Exceptions are: Bahnhof Zoo: Monday to Saturday 6am-midnight; Sundays and public holidays 8am-midnight.

Kreuzberg's colourful Turkish Market.

Airport Tegel: Monday to Friday 7am-9pm; Saturdays, Sundays and public holidays 8am-8pm.

Stamps can be purchased at post offices and from the yellow machines located next to some postboxes, which are also painted bright yellow.

The major post offices also offer fax services.
See also **Telephones**

Public Holidays

New Year's Day: 1 January
Epiphany: 6 January
Good Friday to Easter Monday
May Day: 1 May
Ascension Day: May
Whitsuntide: May
Unification Day: 3 October
All Saints' Day: 1 November
Christmas Day: 25 December
Boxing Day: 26 December

Public Transport see Transport

Religion

Information about church services in the city can be obtained on ☎ **(030) 0 11 57**.
See **Tourist Information Offices**

Smoking

In general this is still widely tolerated in the city, although the trend is gradually changing. Smoking is prohibited on public transport and in certain public buildings but is common in bars and restaurants; there may be some non-smoking areas.

Stamps see Post Offices

Taxis see Transport

Telephones

Local and long-distance calls can be made from all post offices and public call boxes. Kiosks accept either coins or, more commonly, phone cards, which can be purchased at any post office and some shops for 12DM, 20DM or 50DM.

As in most countries, telephone calls made from hotels may be more straightforward and convenient but they are more expensive.
To call Germany from abroad, ☎ **00 49** (+ area code)
The international dialing code for Berlin is ☎ **00 49 30**
Operator: ☎ **0 3**
Directory enquiries: ☎ **11 833**
International enquiries: ☎ **11 834**
Telegrams: ☎ **0 11 31**
Country codes are as follows:
Australia: ☎ **00 61**
Canada: ☎ **00 1**
Ireland: ☎ **00 353**
New Zealand: ☎ **00 64**
UK: ☎ **00 44**
USA: ☎ **00 1**

Time difference
Berlin is on Central European time, one hour ahead of GMT.

Tipping
Tips are not automatically expected and can be added to the bill at your discretion – usually about 10 per cent. Only occasionally will service have already been included. A small gratuity is usually added to taxi fares.

Tourist Information Offices
Tourist Information Centres bear the international '**i**' symbol and are usually open during normal office hours. There are five main offices of Berlin Tourismus Marketing (BTM) GmbH in the city: the central tourist hotline for all enquiries is ☎ **(030) 25 00 25**.

- Europa-Center, Budapester Strasse; open Monday to Saturday 8am-10.30pm.
- Brandenburger Tor, Pariser Platz; open daily 10.30am-7pm.
- Tegel Airport, main hall; open daily 5.15am-10pm.
- Info-Point Dresdner Bank, corner of Unter den Linden and Charlottenstrasse.
- KaDeWe (Department Store of the West), U-Bahn Wittenberg Platz.

German National Tourist Offices abroad can be contacted at the following addresses:
Australia Lufthansa House, 12th Floor, 143 Macquarie Street, Sydney 2000 ☎ **(0123) 673890**
Canada 175 Bloor Street East, North Tower, 6th Floor, Suite 604, Toronto, Ontario M4W 3R8 ☎ **(416) 968 1570**
UK 65 Curzon Street, London W1Y 8NE ☎ **(0171) 495 0081**
USA 122 East 42nd Street, Chanin Building, 52nd Floor, New York, NY 10168 0072 ☎ **(212) 661 7200**
11766 Wiltshire Boulevard, Suite 750, Los Angeles CA 90025 ☎ **(310) 575 19799**

Tours
Berlin Tourismus Marketing GmbH (*see* **Tourist Information Offices**) offers themed city tours especially for groups. Choices include *Jewish Life and History, The Cold War* and *Prussian Jewels*.

BTM also runs bus tours of the city, with different focuses. For example, *Baroque Berlin, Development of the Government Quarter* or *Kreuzberg*.

With over 600km of waterways flowing through Berlin's central district, boat trips are an ideal way to see the city's sights and there are many options on offer, including overnight excursions and evening tours.

Transport

Public transport in Berlin is comprehensive and efficient. Information, maps and timetables can be obtained from the local transport authority, Berliner Verkehrsbetriebe (BVG), BVG-Pavilion Hardenbergplatz, in front of Zoo Station; customer service open 6am-11pm daily ☎ **(030) 752 70 20**.

Various types of tickets for different periods of time are available, ranging from a single ticket valid for two hours to weekly tickets. All are valid and interchangeable on the entire BVG network, which includes U-Bahn, S-Bahn, bus and tram systems. Tickets are obtainable from the yellow or orange automatic machines at U-Bahn and S-Bahn stations, as well as ticket offices.

Children under 14 travel at reduced rates; children under six travel free.

The light and spacious Europa-Center shopping arcade is full of refreshing greenery.

The **WelcomeCard** for Berlin and Potsdam allows unlimited travel on the transport network, for one adult and three children, for three days. It costs 29DM and also allows a discount of up to 50 per cent on certain attractions and tours. The **24h WelcomeCard** offers the same discounts for a 24 hour period. Cards are available from tourist information offices, ticket offices and many hotels.

Train: There are two urban rail networks: the **S-Bahn** (Stadtbahn/city train), and the **U-Bahn** (underground). Trains run on the S-Bahn approximately every 10 minutes and on the U-Bahn every five minutes; at weekends, U-bahn lines 1, 9 and 15 operate through the night. Contact the German Railway Information Office ☎ **(030) 312 10 42** (open Monday-Friday 8.30am-6.30pm, Saturday until 1pm).

Bus: Cream-coloured double-decker buses link the two rail networks and there is a good night service; the exit doors are at the back of the bus. Single tickets only are sold on buses and trams; others must be purchased in advance from a machine.

Taxi: Taxi stands can be found at the airport and throughout the city, or by calling ☎ **(030) 690 22**, **(030) 26 10 26**, **(030) 21 01 01**, **(030) 21 02 02** or **(030) 96 44**.

Tram: Currently operating in eastern Berlin; there are plans to extend the service in western Berlin; tickets are available as for buses.

Ferry: BVG operates a number of ferry services in the Wannsee and Köpenick areas.

TV and Radio

Berlin has six main TV channels, and cable and satellite television is available in many of the larger and more expensive hotels. Programmes listed as OF in the newspapers will be in their original language – usually English/American and French.

English-speaking radio channel: BBC World Service (90.2 FM).

Berlin Radio mainly features music programmes.

Vaccinations

see **Before You Go p.112**

Youth Hostels

see **Accommodation p.97**

INDEX